Life in the Suburbs

Growing up near Watford in the 50s and 60s

Dave Taylor-Jones was born in Carpenders Park, near Watford and worked most of his life as a chartered structural engineer in the oil and gas sector. He left England in 1970 and has lived and worked abroad in Belgium, Holland, Germany and Australia. Since 1980 he has settled with his wife and family in the South of France, near Nice. He has written memoirs, poetry, and specialises in short story fiction.

Also by Dave Taylor-Jones:
Another Side of France

Life in the Suburbs

Growing up near Watford in the 50s and 60s

Dave Taylor-Jones

Matador
9 Priory Business Park,
Wistow Road, Kibworth Beauchamp,
Leicestershire. LE8 0RX
Tel: 0116 279 2299
Email: books@troubador.co.uk
Web: www.troubador.co.uk/matador
Twitter: @matadorbooks

ISBN 978 1789018 820

British Library Cataloguing in Publication Data.
A catalogue record for this book is available from the British Library.

Printed and bound in the UK by TJ International, Padstow, Cornwall
Typeset in 11pt Minion Pro by Troubador Publishing Ltd, Leicester, UK

Matador is an imprint of Troubador Publishing Ltd

This book is dedicated to my brothers,
Steve and Vic.

Contents

Back to the Beginning

I was about ten years old when I found an old brown leather case, small and of unusual proportions, up in the attic of my mum's house. I brought it down to show to her. It was wintertime and there had been a problem with the water tank inside the roof – she thought it was frozen so she asked me to go up and check it – it wasn't the sort of job she wanted to do.

My parents had bought their bungalow in 1937 at Carpenders Park, which is situated halfway between Harrow and Watford and had just about got it straight when the Second World War started. My father, Albert George Taylor (who my mother preferred to call Dave), joined the 79th Armoured Division, Royal Corps of Signals, 21st Army Group at the beginning of the Second World War on March 5th 1940. He had been an assistant chemist with Boots before the war, but his hobby was building and using radio sets, so he was probably pleased to join the Signals Corp. I presume this was because it allowed him to do something he liked and understood. He was stationed in the UK from 1940 until 1944 and his regiment was moved around to different homeland locations during the war, seemingly always in the north of the country. For much of this time my mother, Olive, did not live at home in Carpenders Park but followed my dad around, trying to find work and lodgings near to where he was stationed. Her longest period away from home was at Byfield, a small town in Northamptonshire near Daventry, where she managed to get a job at Byfield Station as a railway ticket office clerk.

My dad became a signal dispatch rider, delivering urgent communications to other Army units. I suppose this gave him a degree of freedom to occasionally divert his motorcycle journeys to see Olive, mostly without notice and often late at night. She did finally have to return home, pregnant with my brother Steve, in 1943 and Dave visited her there whenever the opportunity arose.

It must have been on one of his last motorcycle visits that he left behind the small brown leather case I had found in the attic. Inside was a series of waxed linen Ordnance Survey maps covering the Midlands and Southern England. These maps are very accurate, some are to small scale, but they are incredibly well drawn. In the war all signposts and town names were removed in order to confuse the enemy, so these maps must have been the only way my dad could have found his way around. When I had my first bicycle, I even used one of the maps on a cycle ride with my brother from Carpenders Park to North Wembley and later, when I was sixteen, I used another one when I rode to Southend and back.

My brother Steve was born in August 1943 and from this time Olive lived permanently at home at Carpenders Park. Dave, however, by early spring 1944 was under canvas on the south coast of England along with hundreds of thousands of other servicemen, awaiting the Normandy invasion. Very fortunately for me, he managed to get a lift back to London in May to stay with Olive, just before the Channel crossing commenced in June. During this brief interlude I was conceived. Olive said goodbye to him on the Sunday evening, with baby Steve in her arms. She never saw him again.

The weather in May was good, but the Allied generals wanted to wait for a full moon and high tide to make the landing on the dangerous beaches of Normandy. Their best possibility was June 6th, but by June 4th the weather was so rough it looked like they would have to abandon their planned invasion date and wait another month – not something easily swallowed by the commanding generals. A slight weather-window possibility presented itself on June 6th and by making the decision to go, the Allied Commander, General Dwight D. Eisenhower, caught the Germans off their guard. Even the German General Rommel was away on holiday visiting his wife and many other German officers did not believe the Allies would risk landing in such weather and had taken leave as well.

Dave landed with his Signal Corps and they made their way with his Division across France and Belgium to Brussels, where he was stationed for a short period. During this time, he managed to send Olive a card for her 30th birthday, July 9th 1944.

From Brussels, Dave's regiment moved behind the advancing British Army units, finally reaching Antwerp in the autumn of 1944 and from here he sent Olive a Christmas card. During the last months Hitler changed his tactics and ordered all V1 and V2 rocket attacks on London to cease. He turned his attention to the important port of Antwerp, the significant landing stage for the Allies' advance into Germany. Over 175 days the Germans fired more than 4000 V1s and 1700 V2s at Greater Antwerp, which later came to be called, 'The City of Sudden Death'.

On December 16th Dave was the only one of his squadron to be off duty and he went to see a new film, *The Plainsman*, at the Cinema Rex in the Avenue de Keyser in central Antwerp. At 3.22pm the cinema received a direct hit from a V2 rocket, launched by the Germans from Enschede in Holland, one hundred and thirty miles away. Five hundred and sixty-seven people were killed, including my father, and 291 were wounded. This was the worst V2 rocket attack in the Second World War and is recorded in the Guinness Book of Records 1958.

The Chronicle of the Second World War makes the following report:

Antwerp 16 Dec 1944

VE ROCKET KILLS 564 IN ANTWERP CINEMA

A VE rocket hit the Rex Cinema in the Avenue de Keyser at 3.20pm today, killing 564 people, including 296 Allied servicemen. They were part of a capacity audience of 1200 watching the popular Buffalo Bill film. There was a flash, then the balcony and ceiling collapsed and the screen tumbled forward. The Germans had switched the main weight of the VE attacks from London to Antwerp because of the Ardennes offensive. Today's rocket came from Enschede in the Netherlands just 130 miles away.

Olive, unaware of this tragic event, received her Christmas card from Dave and passed Christmas at home in Carpenders Park with her son Stephen. Normally she would have been informed of her husband's death by letter from the War Office. However, this letter was not sent to the correct address, the house number was omitted in error and it was a personal letter from Dave's commanding officer Major D. H. Strange which informed her of her husband's passing.

My brother Steve was sixteen months old when his dad was killed. I was born on February 11th 1945, almost two months later.

Our mother did not talk much to us about our father when we were young children. We grew up knowing he was killed in the war – but we knew little more than that.

Although it must have been difficult for her to raise her little family after this tragedy, she was a wonderful mother to us. When we were small, we were lucky to have her all to ourselves. I think she was so hurt by Dave's death, she found a place in her head to lodge her loss and managed not to externalise to other people how devastated she was.

She stoically began to bring up two children in war-exhausted England in the second half of the 1940s, with little money apart from a war widow's pension. There must have been hundreds of thousands of families in the same situation, not just in the United Kingdom but throughout Europe. We forget in times of peace how war completely shatters people's dreams of the future by killing their loved ones. In the course of time the lost one's physical form grows faint in our memories and, eventually, they are forgotten and eased into the past, as new families are made and only faded photographs and mementoes are kept. The dead become just a name in the upper reaches of a family tree and it is the present that marches forward, with its daily exigencies, wrapping us up in its details. Perhaps this is life's way of protecting us from dwelling too much on our loss for too long, which might plunge us into depression. Olive married again in 1950 and had two more children, so for her the realities of a busy life kept the sad memories of her loss at bay.

My dad was buried at Schoonselhof Cemetery, Antwerp, but Olive never visited her husband's grave. She even came to see me when I lived in Brussels in 1970, when she was fifty-six years old, but I never thought to ask her where my dad was buried and if she wanted to go to visit him there. I must have been so involved in my own life I never thought to broach this sensitive subject with her. I think she avoided mentioning his death, maybe it was almost taboo for her. Perhaps she did not know how I would react to it. Maybe she felt some guilt on her side for bringing a child into the world without a father. Who knows the answers to these difficult questions? Anyway, it is all too late now.

This case of maps is about the only thing I have from my father now, apart from his medals and a pair of his boots. I decided to find out more about the maps and after researching the Internet I took them to a specialist map shop in George Street, in the West End of London. Mr. Jonathan Potter sells maps much older than the ones I showed him, but he looked them over with some interest.

"These aren't my area of expertise," he said, "you should take them to Maggs, dealers in rare books and manuscripts, in Berkeley Square – they have a military map department."

Well, there is nothing my wife and I like to do more when we are visiting London, than to walk around Mayfair. On a rainy afternoon we fetched up at Maggs, which is in a beautiful sandstone brick building. Ancient books line their floor to ceiling bookshelves and on being greeted by two charming young assistants, we explained the maps' provenance.

"We need Hugh," they said. Hugh eventually appeared and looked over the maps.

"Hmm, no military installations are shown," he said, "which would make them more interesting. But the colours are superb for seventy years old and the level of detail is fascinating. They're not worth much though."

Well, that was fine with me, I only wanted to find out more about them – they definitely were not for sale.

I did finally visit Schoonselhof Cemetery with my brother Steve in July 2009 in order to honour our father's death. I think I would have loved him and it has always seemed unfair I never had that chance. I've missed being able to chew things over with a father, especially when difficult decisions were to be made. Through this visit, late as it was, I felt a door which had been open throughout my life could now be closed.

I have written this collection of stories to keep the door open a little longer, capturing some of the early parts of *My Life in the Suburbs*.

St. Blaise, France, February 2019

Music Lessons

In 1955 I used to ride my bicycle, which had been bought for £2 from a boy up the road, into Watford for my music lessons. These were on Tuesday afternoons at 3.30pm which meant I left St. Meryl Primary School three quarters of an hour earlier than normal. I think this shorter school day positively influenced my early feelings about wanting to learn the piano.

Mr. Graves lived in a road called Carey Place, which was just past Rossi's Ice Cream Bar in the High Street. It was a narrow road at first, suddenly turning a sharp right angle to reveal a little street of mostly terraced houses.

Number 82 was not a terraced house but stood alone, and I used to wheel my bike up the path and ring the bell of the side door. While I waited for an answer, I took my music case off the bike's crossbar and sheltered under the porch from the rain, which often used to soak the bottom half of my short trousers, making them dark grey and crinkly.

Mr. Graves would let me in and say, "Hello," through his moustache. The house smelt old. No other house I knew smelt like this one, a dusty old smell which now somehow reminds me of blue and white china, Chinese paintings, umbrella stands and dark curtains.

The house wasn't from my lifetime at all – it was something I had missed. I am sure in times gone by women had thrown tea parties there, worn their long dresses with tassels, danced the Charleston and had a gay time.

Mr. Graves would show me through to the room facing the street, which was his living room. Winnie, his tabby cat, used to quickly jump up to sit on the warm piano stool as soon as it was vacated. Graves loved to pretend to cuff him and the cat would run to the scullery looking guilty.

I would sit on the stool before the upright piano and unload my music case, which was always a source of bother. The damn thing never closed properly and many times I had to collect the sheets of music off the road or, in this case, his floor.

Graves was old, very old. About eighty, I think. He used to examine my report book and look at the exercises he had written there the week before which were meant for me to practice on our piano at home. Then came the big rigmarole of playing it all. I used to learn the music by heart, in order to be able to watch my fingers while I played, instead of reading the music. We would go through all the scales, major and minor, then the set pieces played from a great thick grey slab of a book called *The Tutor*. I'd play a piece, he'd criticize it and then show me my next exercise.

When he played, his yellow hands flicked over the dirty ivory keys and he'd be singing out the notes all the time. The veins on his hands stood high and proud, pumping blood to fingers which seemed more alive than the rest of him.

At four o'clock he used to make tea for us on a gas stove in the kitchen. While he was away, I would stroke the cat and play with the metronome. Gas lights shone outside in the streets where it was already getting dark. I would think about the journey I would have to make riding home, when it felt so cold cycling in my short trousers.

He would put teacups on a table next to the piano and talk about composers, making dreams for me. His eyes went away sometimes, gazing into some place in the distance and when he had a clear memory his voice would bark excitedly and he'd spit in my face with his words. I didn't mind, I loved him.

The first time I came to play I was nine years old. When I did something wrong, he used to say "Oh no, Oh no, no, no," and then I used to cry. He never became angry or shouted, perhaps he was just disappointed I wasn't his grandson, who might have had his gift for playing the piano.

My friend, Jim, used to have his lesson before me. Jim was two years older than me, much taller, with a mop of ginger hair and freckles. If I was early for my lesson Jim would still be having his, so I would have to sit and wait in a leather armchair in the hall. Poor Jim, he'd play his best, then Graves would say, "Now, James, let's try it again from the last rest."

Jim would give an exaggerated sigh and, although I couldn't see him, I could imagine his big shoulders lifting and his hands wanting to flatten ten notes at once.

When I was eleven years old, I changed schools. I started at secondary school in Watford and would often pass Carey Place when I walked up the High Street. But I didn't have my piano lessons there any more, for one day in summer a man had knocked on our front door and said Mr. Graves had died. I was a bit upset and wondered what had become of his cat Winnie.

I then transferred to the Watford School of Music and lost all interest in the piano. Now, when I remember the lessons there, it seems it was always winter. I can't recall a summer playing the piano.

I remember cycling home to Carpenders Park from those lessons in Watford. It was fine cycling back down the High Street hill, up through Oxhey to Watford Heath, but when I reached Oxhey Lane there were no street lights at this time. My bicycle lights were so weak I expected to be hit by a car from behind at any minute. After a while I used to ride on the footpath for safety's sake. In the dips in the road, Scotch mist used to lie, frosty cold, making me hold my breath. My legs were chapped by the wind and at each turn of the pedals they rubbed the music case, which was strapped to the bicycle's crossbar. I used to see vague monsters in the hawthorn bushes and I was glad to see the bright lights of St. Meryl Estate, welcoming me to where we lived. I used to save some chewing gum or a sweet for when I reached the top of Carpenders Avenue which was lit by the estate road lights. I suppose they were like a reward for pedalling so hard through the darkness of the main road behind me.

Nothing seemed important then, just the knowledge of a coal fire at home, some hot buttered toast, my mother and her warmth. She'd hold me to her, my face pressed into her chest, ask me about my lessons and look at the report Mr. Graves had written about my efforts. With her dreaming of me playing before hundreds packed into town halls and saying to the people sitting next to her, "That's my son," I'd smile a special smile I kept only for her.

Christmas Times Past

In England, there is something magical about the end of the month of December, for as Christmas starts to get nearer, there is an increased awareness that the old year is finishing and a new one is about to begin. When I was little, I thought Christmas Day was the last day of the year and Boxing Day was the first day of the New Year. It was only when we began visiting some friends for New Year's Day that I realised my mistake and understood there were more days before December was finished.

There was so much excitement at the coming of Christmas. It was not just the prospect of receiving presents, but more the idea of having something to look forward to. It began with the rehearsals for the school play with my part's dialogue underlined in red, to help me learn my lines. Then, from the second week of December, carol singers would come around our bungalow estate at Carpenders Park. They were often little kids who knocked at our door and began singing only when it was opened. My mum always gave them a threepenny bit, whether they sung well or not. I remember writing when I was a teenager:

Christmas Callers

> *Two more cards arrived today*
> *A little boy was turned away*
> *Carol singing at the door*
> *This lad's been here five times before…*

The local church choir had about thirty singers who used to walk around the estate and sing carols while grouped together in the middle of the road. They sang well and you could easily hear them from inside your house. We went out into the damp, foggy evening air to hear them better and put pennies into their collection box.

I think my first memories of Christmas are when I was five years old. My mother would bring out the Christmas decorations box, which held amongst other things rolls of red and green streamers. The red was bright pillar box red and the green the emerald colour of Christmas tree branches. She twisted these streamers together to make a fat red and green rope which she suspended from the picture rails in our lounge. It was fixed with drawing pins along its length, so it would hang in neat loops. There were also lantern decorations which were packed flat, but you could spread them apart with a fan-like movement and they became lanterns of coloured paper we could hang up. They were a bit delicate but I loved them.

My mum also bought kits of coloured paper for us to make paper chains. These came in the form of little books of different coloured strips about 15 cms long by 2.5 cms wide and were gummed at one end. My mum, my brother Steve and I would sit together at the kitchen table, peel off a strip and then make it into a ring by licking the gum and sealing the ends in a circle. The next link in the chain was made by choosing a different colour and threading it through the first link and closed as before. The chain grew longer until it was about three metres in length and ready to be suspended from the kitchen ceiling. The decorations changed the aspect of our little bungalow completely. We were enchanted.

Mum had saved some old Christmas tree decorations from before the war and she would buy a small Christmas tree and decorate it. These were little glass Chinese lanterns, in yellow, orange, light blue and white. They had torch bulbs inside them which were supposed to light up, running off a battery. We could never make them work and had no dad to fix them. We put them on the tree anyway.

We also had some silver icicles made of thin sparkly wire, which dropped into shape when they were dangled on the Christmas tree. Then finally, lametta shreds were draped on the branches so in the dark of the lounge, with only the light of the coal fire and the electric street lights from outside, the room took on a new and magical aspect.

My brother Steve and I hung up our socks on Christmas Eve and when we woke up on Christmas morning, we were delighted to find them filled with marbles, oranges, little games and chocolate sovereigns covered in gold paper. During the latter part of the forties most people could not afford much more than this, so I think it was what most working-class children traditionally received.

We posted our letters to Father Christmas up the coal fire chimney in the lounge, hoping like mad we would get a tricycle or scooter. I remember one time when Steve's letter fell down and burnt up quickly in the flaming coals. His chin dropped as he thought his wishes were lost. My mum quickly improvised, "Don't be silly Stephen, Santa will read them in the smoke!" So that was alright then.

Some years later, after my mum remarried and twins Victor and Vanessa were born in 1951, Christmas became more elaborate and even more exciting. New modern paper decorations were bought but we always used the red and green streamers too. The tension built up over the days with our parents shopping and bringing home parcels which were stored away in the bottom of locked wardrobes. The week before Christmas, on a Saturday afternoon, we had our trip to Watford to visit Father Christmas in Cawdells department store. Here you sat on Santa's knee and he asked you what you wanted for Christmas and enquired if you had been good during the past year. After receiving a small gift, you could then run through Santa's Grotto of white cotton-wool winter scenes with a few tired-looking stuffed penguins.

Stan, my mum's new husband, was from Yorkshire and he had different traditions to ours. He immediately instituted a large Christmas Eve dinner for his close family and Olive, my mum, would spend an enormous time preparing for it by cooking his favourite dishes. These were mostly cold meats like brawn, hams, scotch eggs and pickles, with salads and savoury desserts. Steve and I were packed off to bed after being presented to various new aunts and uncles – it was not an evening for kids.

On Christmas Eve, 1950, Olive and Stan had a successful evening dinner and they probably did not get to bed until after midnight, after having done all the washing up and clearing away. They placed our stockings, full of all sorts of toys, at the end of our beds and retired for a well-earned night's sleep. Unfortunately, we woke up at about 2am and were so excited with Father Christmas's gifts we started to play with them immediately. If I remember rightly mine included a small plastic trumpet and a little drum, so we were soon heard by our parents in the room next door. Olive and Stan were not amused to be woken up so quickly after just going to sleep and we were told off sharply and the stockings removed.

The next morning, we woke up and there were our stockings at the end of our beds. But when we investigated, we found they were full of coal and sticks of wood to start the fire!

Our hearts sank, where were our real stockings?

With tears in our eyes we went in to see our mother and asked to have our real stockings. She was not very forgiving and it was only after a gloomy breakfast that she relented and gave us the ones Father Christmas had brought for us. I remember this Christmas now and can only wonder what their Protestant souls were trying to instil in two innocent children of five and seven years. Did we deserve such a shock?

As the fifties progressed my parents could afford to buy us more expensive presents and Victor and Vanessa joined the paper chain production in the kitchen. Every year we were all bought a special big present, like roller skates or cowboy guns, which we received after breakfast in the lounge. We always had our Christmas dinner at lunchtime around two o'clock. With Stan's salary from the Sun Printers in Watford, they could afford much better fare and we normally had the English roast lunch with a turkey. Stan always bought a bottle of Barsac white wine which many years later, when I was allowed to taste it, I discovered was quite sweet. My mum would make a large Christmas pudding and would hide a silver threepenny bit inside it for a lucky person to find. We had the pudding with custard, although in later years we changed to cream. After lunch, we would help mum wash up and we'd all join in together singing carols. Then she would listen to the Queen's speech at 3pm.

After this we sat around the coal fire in the lounge and gave out the presents which we had bought for one another. Steve and I received sixpence a week pocket money from our parents, some of which we used to save, so nearer to Christmas we could buy everyone little gifts. After we were eleven years old, we both used to earn money doing a paper round every morning, so then we could afford to buy more expensive presents. Usually we went to Boots the Chemist in Watford to buy mum a packet of bath salts or talcum powder. For Stan, we would usually buy a screw-driver or some useful tool for his garage.

At Christmas, there were always invitations to friends' and relatives' houses for drinks, and for teenagers there were lots of parties to go to. Dance halls, like the Trade Union Hall and the Top Rank in Watford had special Christmas evenings. All this gave you so much pleasurable anticipation and the 25th of December became the centre of attraction.

On Christmas morning, when we were older, we had our friends call on us at home to drink a toast to Christmas. We always put up holly which we gathered from trees on nearby Old Redding hill and had mistletoe to be kissed under.

Fifty years ago, I wrote the poem below, which was a little girl's Christmas list to Santa Claus.

Lucy's Christmas List, Christmas 1965

Dearest Santa, please excuse
This little note, for we would choose
A rocking horse for little Kevin,
Not too big, he's only seven,
Two six guns, a big wigwam
Two sheriff badges if you can.
Cheyenne Bodie too, I hope,
He's my very own dreamboat.

A cricket bat, football and stuff,
A life-size Yogi-Bear's enough
For Gillian who lost a tooth,
It grows again is that the truth?
Please can you send me a blue ribbon?
Two teddy bears called Titch and Biggun'.
A new doll's house, a tennis ball
A painting book, oh that's for Paul

Who comes to play on rainy days.
A dozen marbles, a doll which says
"Mama" when she's upside down
And don't forget my new ball gown
Just like Mummy's – very long,
A puppy too, if that's not wrong
With Daddy, who's not here right now,
He's working late and that is how,

I'm all alone to write to you.
Please I'm sorry that the flue
Of our chimney's very small
It's so sooty, dark and all.
Now I'll send this Christmas Letter,
Hoping Rudolph's nose is better.
I wonder how you find this list,
Posted up the chimney twist.

Why don't the flames burn it away?
Mummy said she couldn't say.
So, all that's left for me to write
Are thanks from me, this Christmas night.

P.S.
A last request from Pete and Bob in
Can they meet Batman and Robin?

Nowadays I wonder if children write Christmas lists and if they do, do they still put them up the chimney? My children did, when we had an open fire. However, I believe this little act increases their anticipation and, surely, this is what Christmas is all about for them – looking forward to things.

In this electronic age, perhaps some enterprising soul has invented an App so a Christmas List can still be written and posted up a virtual chimney to Father Christmas.

If they have, perhaps today's Lucy might have written the following:

Lucy's Christmas List, *Christmas 2015*

Dearest Santa, please excuse
This little note, for we would choose
A red skate board for little Kevin,
Not too fast, he's only seven,
Two MP3s of One Direction
"Up All Night" is my selection
Liam Payne would do (I hope),
He's my very own dreamboat.

A robot puppy, Lego and stuff,
A Miffy Lamp would be enough
For Gillian who lost a tooth,
It grows again is that the truth?
I'd love Rio Rollers of my own,
And those snazzy Beats Headphones
Jurassic Park – Blue Ray 3D
Robot Transformers, they're for Steve.

He lives next door and is asking for
One of those Razor Ground Force cars.
For me a Princess Phone I think,
In my favourite colour pink,
Barbie's Colour Change bag, oh zoot!
Two Furby Booms, they are so cute.
My mummy's promised me a kitten,
But it's a long shot, I'm admittin'.

With my dad, who's not here right now,
He's working late and that is how,
I'm all alone to write to you
On my I-Pad, if that's not too
Electronic, for I'm sure that
You will use the new Chimney App.
It looks like a virtual chimney flue
Just add this list and click it through.

Now I'll send this Christmas Letter,
Hoping Rudolph's nose is better.
I'll press the button on my Pad
Knowing old Santa will be glad
With my list in digi-format
How could he improve on that?
So, all that's left for me to write
Are thanks from me, this Christmas night.

P.S.
A last request, I'm so sure you'll moan
But do you think I could have a Drone?

Steam or Smoke

I knew Eddie forty years ago when we worked together at Teddington in Middlesex. He was an intelligent, practical engineer and we worked closely for about eight months on the design of a drainage project for a large housing contractor. He was a small man with a great sense of humour, a wicked smile and a long, dirty laugh.

Like most men, we took our time getting to know one another, but over a beer and steak and kidney pie in the pub opposite the office I learnt he was thirty-two years old and married with a little boy. Eddie had a lifelong passion which I discovered was trains. In the 1950s, before the expanded electrification of the British railway network, steam trains were the kings. It was these wonderful engines, which were both the workhorses and the racehorses of our railways, that Eddie worshipped.

I learnt about his love for trains in a strange way, because perhaps not evident to everyone, engineering is basically all about numbers. For example, all engineering drawings are numbered, so they can be traced and recalled when needed. One day we were sorting through a drawing register, checking off which drawings were finished and what was missing – a sort of status check. Suddenly, Eddie said something like, "*46225 – Duchess of Gloucester*" and afterwards, for almost all of a certain range of numbers, he starting quoting engine names. Now, when I was a kid, I had spotted trains and collected their numbers, but for me it was just a craze which had not outlasted my ninth year, so I understood what he meant and found it amusing. Eddie, I then realised, was train mad.

When Eddie was a kid, he would spend every available hour train spotting, filling up his *Ian Allan Locospotters* book with witnessed sights of steam engines. He lived at Wembley, where the London Midlands Region trains passed through on their way from London up through England and on to the North and Scotland. He spent hours of his young life in the drizzling rain on station platforms, waiting for trains. When he saw them, he'd underline their numbers in pencil in his Spotters Book. The *Locospotters* book listed only steam trains that ran on particular sections of the UK railway network and you were required to be honest, only underlining a train number if you'd actually seen it. The express trains were the gems, the most valuable 'spotting', as they had not only numbers but names as well, like *Duchess of Gloucester*. He must have spent hours on windy stations waiting to be engulfed in the roar of a train passing, sitting in the dirty white smoke, smelling the train disappearing in a clatter of wheels and carriages. So often, as I knew, the train that had passed was the one you had already noted, yet somehow for him, the expectation of seeing a new one was enough to endure rain, cold and, what I found to be, enormous boredom!

But for Eddie there was no ennui, he was in his element. He went through his teens travelling around his area collecting train numbers until by the age of fifteen, he had completed his book and spotted every train which could possibly be included in his special edition. He then got into travelling to goods sheds and had mapped out the layout of famous train yards in great detail. I had never found such a complete pre-occupation with a hobby, which endured with him as a consummate passion well into his mid-twenties. By this time the uglier diesel trains were supplanting the old steam trains and later overhead electrification began to bring an end to the steam era and also to his love.

I thought a lot about his train spotting and we both agreed he'd been lucky not to have been born much later, as it all would have been too late, the steam trains would have been over before he would have seen them all.

It was this which reminded me of my own youth spent growing up near the same London to Midlands railway line. The back garden of our bungalow at Carpenders Park led onto a spinney, which bordered a deep railway line embankment.

Every house had a back fence and installed in ours was a gate, through which my brother and I escaped to play in what became our most important domain. When you're seven and nine years old, woods take on a different meaning. Trees are there to be conquered and our spinney, which topped the railway embankment, was full of seventy-year-old oaks, birches, beech trees and also smaller hazel and elderberry trees. The lower level bracken and bushes made dense foliage for us to play in. We shared this spinney with birds and learnt about their plumage, nests and eggs. I was given *The Observer's Book of British Birds* for my birthday and it became my best companion, only to be equalled by its complement *The Observer's Book of Birds' Eggs*.

In this little wood we named our favourite trees the Catapult Tree, the Silver Birch, the Big Tree, the Ship Tree and they were all landmarks to us, like mountains or hills were to others. They were to be climbed, conquered and enjoyed in all sorts of weather. We sat high up in them as the rain splattered on their leaves and on our heads. Our hands and clothes got filthy from the years of smoke which had drifted up from the trains and been deposited on their bark and branches. We swayed in the branches in strong winds, pretending we were pirates in the rigging during a storm and sat up high in them on glorious summer evenings trying to see further than we had ever walked. These trees lifted our lives from British post-war poverty to a golden future which beckoned from just around the corner.

During these fabulous moments, the trains would puff through the deep embankment, emitting their steam and smoke. The steam billowed across the tracks and disappeared quickly, especially in summer. The smoke was much stronger and we preferred it, even though if we gulped it down, we ended up coughing our guts up. It smelled like a dirty visit to another land of sulphur and dust. It wasn't entirely unpleasant, but it clung to our hair and clothes. We loved it and enjoyed how everything was different and hidden for a short time in the smoke and steam. When enjoying these moments, we were happily unaware this is what makes childhood so precious – the innocence of time passing without you being aware of it.

With our friends from neighbouring homes, we entered into a different life when we were out in the spinney. Parents, with all their orders and control, were left far behind and forgotten. We built our own homes in specially selected sites in the spinney and on the grass-covered embankment. These spots were chosen with care for their views, the beauty of their aspect and usually they were naturally hidden or concealed by us.

In the summer, wild strawberries would appear on the embankment and we would gather them and gorge ourselves, taking home just a few for our families. Lying deep in the grass we felt hidden among the grass stems. Time passed as we'd watch the trains puff by, lost in trying to identify wild flowers with *The Observer's Book of Wild Flowers*. Harebells were my favourite, their fragile blueness seemed to touch my heart and only the sky could compare with their colour. Later I met a girl, when I was about nineteen, whose eyes were the nearest thing I had seen to the colour of those harebells and if I remember correctly, she also made me steam a bit.

Once the summer sun had started to turn the embankment's long grasses blonde, we would start to make our bivouacs from them. They were constructed on the slopes of the embankment out of vertical sticks with twines of grass woven in them, like the crude beginnings of huts. They never got to be very high, with roofs made for them in the same way, under which we crawled to hide and watch the trains go by.

People used to look out of the train windows, point at us and wave as they passed. Inside the camps it was a different world. The sun came in and made sharp patterns of light and although it was almost impossible to turn around – they were so small – you felt at home because you had made them yourself. You were safe.

Except sometimes, sparks from the trains would ignite the dry summer grass, causing us to fight fierce battles to stop the fire spreading and destroying our new homes. Sometimes we won, but often we simply weren't there but at school and returning after 4pm we'd find our play area black and devastated. This was a catastrophe, but we knew next year we could do it all again, at least until we grew up.

It's strange, but all the time we played in this spinney and on the embankment, we were aware of how the trains represented an incredibly strong physical force. We knew they were very dangerous and powerful. Their noise and vibration were, if you went down to the bottom of the embankment, almost unbearable. We were not stupid – to cross those tracks posed a terrible danger. Five lines of standard gauge line were a lot to take into account, not to mention the double tracks of electrified line the red Bakerloo trains ran on. These Bakerloo line trains were little red worm-like trains serving the far reaches of the London commuter system and they ran by picking up their electric voltage from a power line between the tracks. I learnt later how they worked on the Direct Current (DC) system pick-up rail, which acts differently to the conductor of the normal Alternating Current (AC) system of electricity, which we use in houses and domestic utilities. If you get a shock from 240 volts AC, by inadvertently touching a live cable, then you are repulsed and, as long as there is nothing to stop you moving back quickly and recoiling from the shock, you might only suffer a short discomfort and slight perming of your hair. But with DC it is different, it is attractive. If you touch the line then you will have great difficulty removing the part of your body in contact. You will be electrified and die from cardiac fibrillation.

Way back then in the 1950s, all this basic science was far into my future. As children, we definitely considered the railway lines very dangerous. However, we did occasionally dare to go down to touch the steam rails and older boys placed pennies on these lines to see what would happen to them when the train wheels rolled over them. Some particularly mad kids crossed the tracks to gain 'lunatic' status, but all this was carefully controlled by look-outs, to be sure no trains were coming at the moment they made their dash across.

My best friend at this time was a boy called Martin, who lived about fifty houses up the road. His parents were school teachers and Martin always seemed to be brighter than everyone else. He could read before he went to school and was quick at learning the multiplication tables, however, I could climb trees higher than him, knew more about birds and their eggs and had much more freedom than he did. His parents didn't even allow him to go to Cubs.

One of our neighbours had a wonderful black and white dog, called Belinda – a ridiculous name – so we called her by her breed, which was Collie. She, Collie Dog, went everywhere with Martin and me, especially when we were playing out on the embankment. This dog was just looking for a bit of company most of the time and wanted to be with us. Her coat was a beautiful patchwork of long fur. She was obedient and intelligent. I thought of her as a close friend.

Next door-but-one was an old lady who kept chickens. One day we were told a fox had managed to enter her hen coop and had attacked and killed all her chickens. So, on this wet afternoon after school, we set off with Collie Dog, excited as hell, wandering the paths of the spinney until we discovered the fox's footprints in the soft mud and we had to run like mad to keep up with Collie, who now had got the fox's scent. How big would the fox be, could Collie Dog kill it and avenge the death of the chickens? We ran through brambles and elderberry copses, following Collie's mad rush right down to the train station, where the spinney ended in allotment gardens. Here we lost the tracks and had to return home with only our desperate frustration at not succeeding.

On the other side of the railway tracks a different world existed. A London County Council estate had been built for families from the East End of London, who had been bombed out during the Second World War and were relocated there in the early 1950s, giving them a completely new environment. The estate was vast and had several schools, shopping precincts, a library and a few pubs. It seemed a foreign land to our young eyes. Sometimes large gangs of kids would appear on the other bank, which was not high like the embankment on our side. They would throw stones and shout taunts at us as we train spotted. Some climbed the fence on their side and started to attempt to cross the lines. However, usually an adult would emerge from a nearby house to bring order and stop them trying to cross the electrified Tube tracks.

One day Martin and I were sitting on some old ant hills on the bank waiting to catch site of the *Royal Scot* which was supposed to come through, when we noticed a crowd of at least twenty LCC kids massing on their side of the line. They started their usual game of name calling and taunting. We just ignored them, but Collie Dog didn't and ran down to the track's edge and started to bark at them. A stone suddenly whizzed into the bank next to us and we saw what this new danger was. Catapults! We were being targeted and the stones started to rain down on us and we became well aware the grassy slopes offered no protection. We retired swiftly to a ditch which ran along the top of the embankment and peeped out. We were safely out of range, but train spotting was over for the day.

Every autumn we would gather hazelnuts and one day, under a nut tree, quite close to our back fence, I noticed a strange metallic fin sticking out of the ground. My brother Steve said not to touch it – it might be a bomb – so we went back down our garden and reported it to our mum. She came and had a look and was horrified. Steve was right – it was unexploded ordnance. She telephoned the police and later in the afternoon we were visited by two men who told us and our neighbours to stay inside while they went to examine it. Fortunately, it was not dangerous and they defused it and brought it down to their car. One of the men explained that during the Second World War, sometimes the Germans tried to bomb the railway and missed. He asked us to be careful and to immediately report any other similar objects we found. My mum told us the house at 100 St. George's Drive had been hit by a bomb in the war and the front part destroyed. This seemed to me to have been a close shave, even though my parents were not living at home at the time.

Our parents decided for safety's sake we should not play anymore in the embankment spinney, so the gate in the back fence was padlocked shut and the spinney and embankment put out of bounds to us.

And was this the end of an era? Well, yes, for a bit, I suppose. After the summer holidays I went to a new school in Watford three miles away and had less time for the lure of the embankment's old magic. But my younger brother, who was six years my junior, was just too keen and later pressed and pressed for permission to go into the spinney and finally the gate was opened up again. By this time, I was sixteen years old and able to point out to my girlfriend the impossibly high tree houses we had built all those years ago. They were still evident in the winter times through the lacework of the branches in the spinney behind the houses. Adolescence and confusion reigned in hailstones and the spinney took a final step back from my life.

Now, fifty years later, the spinney and embankment are covered thickly with trees sometimes right down to the edge of the train tracks and the whole era of childhood now lies beneath them and also deep within my heart.

The Paper Round

Every day at 5.30am our round, green, metallic alarm clock would ring and Steve and I would get up. Steve, my older brother, had been doing this for a year already, while I had the luxury of lying in bed until 7.30am and then getting up to go to school. Steve, being older, was the first to have a paper round delivering newspapers for Farr's Newsagents on the housing estate at Carpenders Park where we lived.

Steve's round was Carpenders Avenue and included a delivery to Brazier's Milk Farm situated on Oxhey Lane and to some other people who lived on their property. His round ran to about one hundred and ten customers, who ordered their newspapers from Farr's and then had the pleasure of reading them over their breakfast before starting their day, thanks to Steve getting up at that unearthly hour to deliver them. Steve explained that the milk farm delivery was conveniently located halfway through his round, as he walked up Carpenders Avenue to Oxhey Lane. The first day when he approached to deliver the newspaper to the farm house, he found his way blocked by a massive Alsatian dog, who lowered his head slightly, ruffled the fur on his back and gave him a terrible growl. Steve was petrified and although he knew the dog was only defending what he saw as his territory, he didn't feel like challenging him. He stood still and waited until fortunately a farm worker appeared and called the dog off.

"Hey, Henry, let him pass. Come forward, young lad, and let him sniff you, after that he'll know you every day and let you pass."

Steve gingerly approached Henry and was formerly introduced by extending his hand to the dog's nose. This was met by a big wag of the tail. After these formalities, Henry accompanied Steve to the cottages and caravans behind the farm to complete the newspaper deliveries. As the years went by, Henry never missed his rendezvous with Steve every morning and eventually took to accompanying him for the rest of the route back down Carpenders Avenue to the paper-shop. One weekend he even followed Steve back home to our house and sat outside our back gate waiting to be introduced to our mum and me. Steve was obliged to get on his bike and take him back to the farm. Mum told us that some days Henry would show up after we had gone to school and give her quite a shock by silently appearing, patiently waiting at the back gate for his mate.

"Shoo, Henry, he's gone to school, be off with you," she would tell him.

When I was twelve years old, I managed to get the newspaper round on the road next to Steve's. My round was mainly Penrose Avenue, with a part of the next road included too, the lower part of Greenfield Avenue – about one hundred and five houses in all. I first started my round in March 1957. The streets were still dark, it was usually raining and the temperatures were around freezing. English winters in the suburbs of London are fairly grim and dull, wet with a damp cold brought by the east or north winds.

Awakened by that alarm clock we would pull on our clothes; I was still in short trousers, no long ones until thirteen by my mother's rules, and without breakfast we would get on our bikes and cycle down the hill to the newspaper shop. We usually arrived at about 5.50am, when the paper delivery van dropped off the newspapers in big bundles tied up with string. Sometimes the van was late or the shop was not yet open and then Derek Clarke, John Nansen, Paul Bitmead, Judy Harding and Steve and I would try and stay out of the rain in the shop doorways, waiting to start work. We parked our bikes beside the road, supported by their pedals pressing down on the top of the kerb.

On these early mornings, the shop was run by a kindly man of about sixty who we called the Guv'nor – I never knew his real name. He had the keys to the shop and opened up while we lifted the newspaper bundles over from the kerb-side and brought them inside. The lights in the shop were not very bright, the Guv'nor would light up his second cigarette of the day and the delivery boys would laugh and curse among themselves as they made up their rounds. On those dark mornings in the neon lights of the shop we must have resembled hobgoblins hopping about.

Each paperboy, or papergirl in Judy's case, had a book for their round which listed their road's house numbers and the corresponding newspapers to be delivered. The book was also arranged into the days of the week, for although the customers took the same newspaper every day, there were magazines that people purchased on certain days which had to be included too. The deliveries for Monday to Thursday were of a similar weight, but Friday was a really heavy day due to the inclusion of the *Radio Times* for BBC radio and television programmes for the next week and later the *TV Times* for Independent Television programmes. These were bulky papers which many people bought and they added greatly to the weight of newspapers in your bag.

Saturday was also quite a heavy day, with weekly magazines and comics included like the *Beano*, the *Dandy*, the *Eagle*, etc. But the heaviest day was Sunday. The British Sunday newspapers are twice their normal weekday size and this increase in weight meant you could only take half of them in one go and then you would have to return to the shop for the second half.

My first day started on a Sunday, a bit later than normal at 7am, as there was no school to attend. It took me ages to write the number of the house on the top of each newspaper and then to stack them in the order of delivery. I took the first lot, placing the papers, as the Guv'nor showed me, into my green, waxed, stiff canvas bag. I set off at about 7.45am.

It was difficult to walk with the laden bag thrown over one shoulder with the open flap to the front. I staggered off, comforted by the thought that it would never be like this for the other days of the week. Slowly the bag emptied of papers and I kept a good eye on the house numbers to be sure that I didn't deliver number 93's to 95. At Carpenders Park roads have odd numbered houses on the left and even numbers on the right, as you progress numerically, so I did the evens on the right side first and eventually at about 8.30am I arrived back at the shop. I was really surprised to see that all the other experienced paperboys had already finished their rounds and that I was only halfway.

I was delighted to see that the Guv'nor had already marked up my second half of the round, so stuffing it in my bag I went off to finish. I finally finished the first day at 9am, found my bike and cycled back home for breakfast. Steve kindly told me that I would soon get the hang of it and that he had memorized the complete round (after a year) and didn't need to actually mark up the newspapers with the house numbers. I would do this too. This saved a lot of time, but even when I had memorized the complete route for all the days of the week, it still required the Guv'nor to let me know of updates and cancellations for me to record them in the book.

If it was just cold and icy, I didn't mind so much – I could get along with this. But when it was pouring with rain, the only solution was to wear a yellow plastic bicycle cape over your clothes, which covered the paper-bag too. This was a dreary soaking wet way for a boy to start his day. The rainwater would run down my collar and soak the top part of my shirt and get into my shoes, requiring a change of shirt and socks to go to school. However, there was no getting out of it, I had to go. I mean, there were twelve shillings and sixpence to be earned at the end of the week.

I quickly got used to the routine of deliveries and found it was not long before I too, could completely memorize my round for all the days of the week. The Monday to Thursday deliveries became a breeze. From

Monday to Friday the important thing was to finish the round in time to get back home for breakfast at 7.15am and then be ready to catch the train to school in Watford. At first this was a bit touch and go for me on Fridays, with the heavy delivery, but I managed it and as I grew a bit more every year, I became stronger and better able to cope with the Friday, Saturday and Sunday heavy days.

It was great getting paid every Saturday. I opened a Post Office savings account and put the money in there to save up for summer holidays, when Steve and I went camping in Cornwall.

At this time the weekly daily newspapers that we delivered were:

- The *News Chronicle* (my mum's paper)
- The *Daily Express*
- The *Daily Mirror*
- The *Daily Sketch*
- The *Daily Herald*
- The *Daily Mail*
- The *Manchester Guardian*
- *The Times*
- The *Financial Times*
- The *Daily Telegraph*
- The *Daily Worker*

The biggest paper was the *Times* and when this was folded up, some letter boxes were just too small for it to go through. The best I could do was to stick it in a bit, so that it hung down outside and hope that it didn't get torn when it fell onto the porch floor. It seemed the people who wanted highbrow papers like this always had letter boxes that were too small. However, the *Mirror* and the *Sketch* were small papers and these sailed in through the letter boxes with a satisfying thump on to the hall floor. Fortunately, it seemed there were not too many people who bought the *Times* in Penrose Avenue – the *Mirror* and the *Express* were by far the most popular.

Carpenders Park is an estate consisting mostly of semi-detached bungalows and nearly all of them had porches to protect their doorways. They also had front and back gardens, so I often had a nice little gate to open to the front garden and a path to the front door. Some people looked after their gardens and the paths would be lined with lovely rose bushes. The only problem with these was that, in the summer, spiders would spin their webs across the path during the night and if he was not alert, the paperboy walked straight into them. The best approach was to remove the newspaper from the bag at the gate, fold it up ready to post and hold it before you like an Olympic Torch to bat the spiders' webs out of the way. Otherwise you could quickly be covered in rather large diadem spiders.

It seems that when the Carpenders Park houses were designed, the front door choice was endless. Every front door seemed to have the letter box in a different place. It could be in the middle, on the side or, worst of all, at the bottom of the door.

One day Steve was so ill that he couldn't get up to do his round, so I had to do it, as well as my own round. This was really asking a lot. I couldn't start any earlier because the newspapers were only delivered at just before 6am. After explaining the emergency to the Guv'nor I raced off on my round, while he marked up Steve's. Then I had to do his round at top speed. At Brazier's Farm, first of all I had to get by Henry, who when I arrived amazingly seemed to know me, and then deliver to the people living in caravans, which nestled under the trees of an old apple orchard and did not have numbers. I managed to find somebody awake who pointed me in the right direction and I made the deliveries as best as I could. Then I raced back to Carpenders Avenue to finish the odd numbers' side. I got back home at about eight o'clock, changed into school uniform, wolfed down my breakfast and raced to catch the train. Happily, we were both hardly ever ill, but I think I remember he returned the favour later, when I was down with the flu.

When I was fourteen years old Judy Harding, who was the same age as Steve, decided that she would call it a day delivering newspapers to Greenfield Avenue and a new girl called Sandra Smith took her place. Sandra did not possess a bike, so the Guv'nor, in all his wisdom, decided that as her round was next to mine, *I* should carry *her* bag up to the start of *her* round. Initially this meant hanging around for Sandra to finish marking up her papers and then putting not only my bag, but also her's onto my bike and pushing it up to the start of our rounds. Sandra seemed to take an age to complete the marking-up task. I wasn't overly pleased to be forced into this gentlemanly gesture. We did not talk, not a word was said. For two years.

Many people had pets at home and I have to say I never had a problem with a cat on my paper round. Dogs were something else though, as they wanted to guard their homes. Some dogs would wait until you placed the newspaper in the letter box and then launch themselves at the inside of the door, with a massive thump, growling and biting and pulling the paper through. The newspaper must have been in tatters every day.

There was one house on my round that was really strange. The complete bungalow was covered in a sort of green ivy creeper, so thick I could not see the tiled roof and the house looked like it was wearing a green canopy as a hat. The creeper extended into the front garden, which was completely overgrown with hazel bushes and other small trees. A narrow tunnel path had been hacked out of the foliage to allow deliveries to be made to the front door. Even in summer, this tunnel was very dark and seemed the ideal place for bats to hang out, fed on an exclusive diet of massive spiders. When I first saw this house, I was quite unnerved and felt like leaving their paper at the gate. But the *Newspaper Boy Rules for Delivery* absolutely prohibited this sort of scared, chicken approach. If someone near this house had been up at 6.45am they would have seen a small newspaper boy clutching his green delivery bag, transform himself into a whirlwind and race at top speed through the gate, slam the *Manchester Guardian* through the letterbox and be back out in about two seconds flat. I don't think I ever got used to it.

The weather changed throughout the year and I have to say that, once the wet winters were over, I really enjoyed being up early in the spring and summer months delivering newspapers. Few people were about, except those men who were off to catch an early train to work. The sun came out earlier every day, the daytime lengthened and the garden lawns used to sparkle with early morning dew. I would watch the garden flowers slowly progressing from the first snow drops and crocuses of March, to the daffodils and hyacinths of springtime and finally all the summer annual plants like purple aubrietia, stocks, gladioli and of course all those English roses making a heavy scent in the early morning. Walking along the street, nipping up the paths to the houses at this time of the day, it seemed that the morning belonged exclusively to me.

Just before Christmas 1958, Steve was amazed to learn that Judy Harding, before retiring from delivering newspapers, had collected over £6 in Christmas tips by making an evening tour of her paper round and wishing her customers Happy Christmas. Steve and I decided to try and see if we were similarly appreciated.

On the evening of December 23rd, I felt some trepidation at the first house on my Penrose Avenue round, as it happened to be Mrs. Hopkins, one of my mother's best friends. I rang the bell and her daughter Marcia appeared and asked what I wanted. "I'm your paperboy and I have come to wish you Happy Christmas," I trotted out glibly. Marcia whisked around and went off into the bungalow to tell her mum and dad. A few minutes later Mr. Hopkins appeared and pressed half-a-crown into my hand. I could not believe it. My smile from ear to ear must have shown him my immense gratitude and mumbling my thanks I backed off the porch step, nearly falling into his pyracantha bushes. After that I was off on a mission. I don't think anyone refused me a Christmas tip for getting up and delivering them their morning newspapers. The amount ranged from sixpence to half-a-crown. Every year I made £4 – £5 in tips. Of course, I never beat Judy Harding's total – she always received the most.

The most difficult house to collect a Christmas tip from was the Ivy Clad Bungalow, which, when I approached it that evening, showed dim lights on in the lounge. The dark path through the jungle garden was very foreboding. Was it worth it? Should I just miss out on this one? I decided to add a new addendum to the *Newspaper Boy Rules for Delivery* on the subject and gathering my wits I blundered up the path, shone my torch on the door and found the bell. I waited trembling in the dark and heard a shuffling approach from someone in the hallway behind the door. The door swung open and a man with a beard peered out from the twenty-watt lighting.

"I'm your paperboy and I have come to wish you Happy Christmas," I stuttered.

"Well, well," he said, "just a minute." He wandered off and came back grinning. "I suppose you don't really like delivering papers to this house, do you? Must be a bit scary on these dark early mornings?"

"It's OK," I said putting on a brave face, "but why don't you trim back the creepers a bit?"

"Well, I was in Burma in the Second World War, lost in the jungle for about a year, escaping from the Japanese forces. I really got to like the jungle, as it looked after me and now, safely back in Blighty, I just love to have this vine covering my house. It makes me feel secure, sort of close to nature. I live alone and like this, I feel more looked after."

He gave me a two-shilling piece and I didn't have the temerity to ask him about the bats. I felt a bit sad for him living alone, but the house didn't scare me anymore. It takes all sorts, doesn't it?

The Tree House

Growing up in the 1950s in a house behind a heavily-wooded, deep railway embankment might not seem an ideal place, but to me, it was a sort of heaven. It was safe because almost nobody ever went there except my brother Steve, me and other neighbours' children. We were aged about ten to twelve years old, so the spinney offered us a play area which was rich in all sorts of possibilities. We could see birds and find their nests. We could spot the numbers of the steam locomotives that chugged or sped along the railway tracks. But most of all it was the trees, which we could climb and conquer, that gave us the most pleasure.

I'm not sure where we got the idea to build a tree house, but it must have been from the Scouts or some library books as we didn't have a television at this time. Perhaps we saw one in a film on a Saturday morning at the Gaumont cinema, in nearby Watford. Never mind, tree houses became a passion for us.

Initially, we decided to build one in a large silver birch tree, which overlooked the embankment and train tracks, so we could be high up and do train spotting at the same time, bliss. The tree was ideal as it was hard to climb the lower trunk, making it difficult for other people to access our future tree house. There was a big branch which hung down to about two metres above the ground, so we made a long pole from a hazel tree to hook over the end of it. We could then pull it down, grasp it and heave ourselves up to clamber along to the main trunk and then climb up the tree. Not easy, but just possible. This was how we initially conquered the tree, but it was too difficult to do every time. As a means of access, it was just not convenient.

Steve came up with a simpler idea. We took some nails from our mum's shed and borrowed her hammer. We banged the nails into the trunk to make small but adequate grips to climb the three metres of the trunk up to the first branches. After an easy climb of another three metres, the tree split into two big boughs. Further up, one branch had some conveniently-positioned lateral branches on it, which we used to attach some timbers to form the horizontal base of the house. This would be a platform to sit on. Sitting on silver birch branches for a long time did strange things to your bum, as you can imagine, so the luxury of a small wooden floor for two, with some side rails to stop you falling out, was perfect.

When the wind blew hard, we were safely ensconced on the platform, high in the crow's nest of the good ship 'Silver Birch', with flailing green and silver leaves, bending and swaying in our make-believe sea storm. When the trains passed, their steamy smoke drifted up the embankment sides into our tree and we could pretend that we were in a fire and choking to death.

However, after a week away at a summer Scout camp we came back to find the tree house gone – someone had climbed up and stolen the timbers. Steve had always been concerned that anyone could climb up to it, which was unacceptable; we had property rights, hadn't we? We needed to find a better prospect, more difficult to climb and hidden from prying eyes.

We spent some time trying to decide which tree to conquer next to make our home in. About four houses further up our street, behind the back-garden fence, was a large ash tree, which we called the Catapult Tree, which split in two quite low down on its trunk. It was quite difficult to climb, but possessed an excellent place about six metres above the ground to easily construct a platform. Unfortunately, we would have been in plain view of the people who owned the house below and we assumed, probably quite rightly, that they would not take too kindly to two boys banging around in a tree so close to the end of their garden.

The next best choice was a huge beech tree just fifty metres from the Silver Birch, again overlooking the railway. This tree, which we called simply the Big Tree, had a trunk of more than one and half metres in diameter. If you can remember your geometry, then its girth must have been pi times the diameter, so about five metres. This huge tree had always defeated our efforts to climb it. Beech trees have very smooth, light grey bark which can be slippery and there were no branches until about five metres from the ground. We admired this mighty beast, it was probably eighteen metres high and easily the biggest tree in the spinney. Short of finding a long ladder to reach the lowest branches, we could not work out how to beat it. So, we left it, ruefully, but content to know that we were too young and not equipped to climb it, a bit like climbers must have felt about Mount Everest before it was conquered.

Much farther down the spinney towards the railway station was a small pond, which we called the Fever Pond. It smelt awful and was always full of scummy water, old bike frames and milk crates. Just before it, a little back from the woodland path, was another beautiful beech tree about fifteen metres high. We had never tried to climb it. As usual there were no lateral branches until four metres above the ground, where a nice strong branch stuck out and dipped downwards, stopping at two metres above the ground. Steve reckoned that if we made a rope-ladder we could somehow attach it to this branch and climb up. But how to get the ladder up there in the first place and how could we attach it?

We bought some jute rope from the ironmongers with our pocket money and made a rope ladder using rungs made from oak branches. We laid out the rope on our garden lawn by running one length of four and a half metres up one side, then turning the top round in a loop and coming back down the other side. This made a rope path in which we then laid out rungs and attached each one with a clove hitch knot on each side. It took quite a long time to get the rungs nice and evenly spaced. Finally, we had a rope ladder that had a loop at the top, which, we explained to our bemused mother, would be slipped over a branch of the beech tree using a long pole. We had eyes on her washing line prop, but she said no – she needed it too badly. So out we went back into the spinney and found a long thin branch about four metres long with a fork at the top.

We had noted a small branch which grew out of the first lateral and was close to the tree's trunk. This, when cut off, would make an ideal peg for the rope ladder. We borrowed Mum's log saw and I helped Steve pull a branch down and with us both heaving on it, I managed to get a grip on a strong part. By lifting my legs up, I could shimmy along underneath it until with a big effort, I managed to swing my body around and get above the branch to crawl up it towards the trunk. I then lowered a rope down to Steve, who attached the saw to it and I hauled it up. I then cut off the selected branch to form an upward slanting peg.

Now the big moment had arrived. Steve got the long pole, hooked the rope ladder over it and easily placed it over the new peg branch. The rope ladder hung down perfectly with the bottom rung clear of the ground. Steve had the honour of being the first boy to climb our ladder. However, this proved to be quite a difficult feat, which we discovered required a specialist technique.

As soon as you had both feet on the bottom rung, the ladder swung in a pendulum motion, which initially was a bit unnerving. We learnt that as we climbed the swinging ladder, we could time our next step up when it swung back to its centre position. Of course, the nearer we got to the top the less it swung, which made it easier. Then we had to make a clever movement to get up onto the branch. Fortunately, there was another branch just above it, which we could grip and hey presto, there you were up in the tree, standing on the first branch. Then we would pull up the ladder and store it. The tree's foliage was so thick that after climbing close to the trunk we just disappeared up into the leaves. No one knew we were there. We investigated the tree slowly and carefully, gaining confidence as we went up higher. At about seven metres the trunk split into four parts – a sort of double catapult. This was a perfect place to position timber beams and create a platform base for our tree house.

It seems strange now, but in 1956 finding wood to make the base was not that easy. Most people warmed their houses with kitchen stoves, lighting them every day with sticks of dry wood, so they were always on the look-out for old wood for this purpose. However, providence was on our side, as one day we were offered a job by a handyman who lived a few doors down the road. He needed our help to clear out someone's back yard before putting up a new shed and there were masses of very useful pieces of old wood just the right size. We asked if we could have some of it and Reg was only too pleased to give it to us.

We hauled up pieces of this wood into our tree and nailed them to the branches, tying them in place first. This formed a platform that we covered with boards and at last we were able to sit comfortably in our tree. We used more wood for framing the sides and then roughly cut pieces of thin plywood to cover them, making side walls. We only did this on three sides, leaving the front open. With the dense foliage you could not see our house from the ground.

Making a roof was much more difficult, but we eventually managed it using another scrap of ply wood. It was wonderful sitting inside, especially when it rained. The soft pitter-patter of raindrops on our roof made us feel secure and homey. We had to be careful climbing down the wet trunk after the rain, as the beech bark became very slippery.

The tree house opening looked out over the path which led through the spinney, down past the Fever Pond and on towards the flatter areas where the embankment receded, nearer to the station. From this vantage point we could see people well before they arrived. Then we would hush ourselves and watch neighbours walking their dogs, oblivious to us spying on them. This was exciting in an illicit sort of way, knowing that we were observing adults without their knowledge.

In the tree house, we stored our catapults and round smooth stones taken from the stream bed, which were our ammunition. In the autumn, the tree produced thousands of beechnuts as its fruit. These have small, light green husks, with slightly spiky surfaces, which you have to break open to find the fruit inside. At this time, there was a chewing gum called *Beechnut*, which cost one penny and contained four peppermint flavoured tablets inside. It was one of our favourites but, even though the *Beechnut* gum had a picture of the beechnut fruit on the outside of its packet, the real beechnuts, much to our disgust, tasted nothing like it. They were very bitter and totally inedible. This was something of a disappointment to us, as we were used to the spinney and the embankment providing well for us in the summer and autumn.

In the summer there were patches of raspberries which had taken root and spread. These were wonderful treasures which, with our mum's help, we would collect and she would serve as desserts at home.

But I think the queen of the embankment's fruits was the blackberry. These grew on large bushes and were sometimes difficult to gather as they grew so high. Mum had an old walking stick and we used this to hook over the high branches and pull them down, laden with gorgeous black fruit. I guess the higher the branch, the more exposure it had to the sun which is why they produced such big, luscious berries. We took colanders and filled them, bringing home as much as six kilograms of fruit. Mum made them into blackberry puddings, blackberry and apple tarts and, of course, blackberry and apple jam.

The first winter after we built our tree house, we weren't surprised to see it stand out as an ugly structure, clearly visible now that all the pretty beech leaves had been blown off by the strong northern and eastern winds. We watched people who walked up our street gaze in amazement at it halfway up the bare tree in the spinney behind their gardens. We said nothing, but I suspect most people must have known it was the work of Olive Jones' boys.

We kept the tree house for about three summers, only using it when we couldn't be seen in its leafy branches. Then a new family bought the bungalow whose garden was closest to it. The beech tree was not right next to their back fence, but twenty metres into the spinney. However, it was big and dominated the end of their garden. Nothing happened that summer, but during the winter the man who'd bought the house, Mr. Hogbin, came to see my mum and asked us to remove the tree house, claiming that it was an eyesore.

He threatened, "Either your sons remove it, or I will."

On chatting this over with our mother, we decided that it would be very interesting to see Mr. Hogbin try to climb up the tree. Mum was on our side, as the tree was not on his property and she didn't like new people trying to throw their weight around. I think she knew that we were out-growing it anyway.

We left it there and noticed that it didn't get removed. I am sure Mr. Hogbin hadn't a clue how to get up the first part of the beech trunk, he didn't exactly look like the climbing type. He had two sons who were unfriendly and remained apart from the other kids in the road. Mum said they were a strict religious family.

As I worked my way through secondary school, the tree house gradually got battered by the winds and bits fell off. First of all, one of the sides disappeared and then the roof. After a snowy period, the complete superstructure finally disintegrated. This must have pleased Mr. Hogbin, for the base platform was no longer visible, except to the trained eyes of Steve and me.

When I was sixteen and in my last year at school, my class had a party at some rooms we hired in the Watford Trade Union Hall, to celebrate the end of school life. I had just bought my first suit, a single-breasted charcoal grey one, selected after much care and shopping with my friend Peter Hancock. I asked a girl to go with me to the party, who lived in a road just off of ours. She was a pretty girl with long curly hair, which I thought was attractive. When we walked home from the train station after the party, I told her the story of the tree house and asked her if she had noticed it. Yes, she had and she'd always harboured a secret wish to climb up and visit it. What a pity that the jute rope ladder had rotted with age and was now gone. A moonlight visit would have been a wonderful end to a perfect evening.

Victoria 1956 – 61

Having been disqualified from attending a Technical or Grammar school, not actually by any lack of intelligence but by the dreaded 'interview' which at that time finalised the eleven-plus exam, I was destined to go to what was reported to be the worst school in Watford, Victoria Secondary Modern School for Boys. Maybe 'worst' is a bit strong, but Victoria had a reputation for being a rather rough school, a breeding ground for Teddy Boys, my mum said.

Situated in Addiscombe Road, behind the Empire Cinema past the end of Market Street, Victoria was a school where boys and girls were separated, there being two large Victorian red sandstone brick buildings. One for girls and one for boys, with over six hundred children in each. The buildings sat next to one another, the girls' school on Addiscombe Road and the boys' school hidden behind it, up a narrow alley bordering a graveyard. The two schools were kept firmly apart by a four-metre high wall, topped by a one-metre high chain-link fence. This was long before the idea of co-educational teaching with boys and girls in the same classroom, which was more generally introduced later in the twentieth century. We were 'boys are boys and girls are girls and never the twain shall meet', except on the waste ground behind the cycle sheds…

Fortunately for me, my older brother Steve was already at the school, two years ahead of me. He and his friends provided valuable protection from the louts of the year just above mine, who couldn't wait to show the new recruits what softies we were. Due to the influx of children born after the war, the so-called Baby Boomer generation, the existing school buildings were not large enough to accommodate my year. The school had to create an additional class, which made five classes in total, with thirty to thirty-five boys in each class, streamed by academic ability. I was in Class 1 (Steve was in Class 3), and below me were Classes 1A, 1alpha, 1B, and 1C. Due to the lack of classrooms, extra single-storey accommodation called 'the New Wing' was used to house us new kids, far away from the Watford town centre, towards Bushey. This required some clever manipulation of the weekly timetable to enable everybody to attend their lessons at the right time, in the correct classrooms.

Previously at primary school I had my own desk in my own classroom, so I could leave all my text books and exercise books in the desk, but at Victoria I did not have a designated classroom in the first year of school. I had to carry my books around with me in my satchel. This required judicious planning every day, as I only wanted to take the books and equipment I needed for that day's study. As first-years we spent about three days a week at the Wing and the other two days, when we had woodwork, music and games, we attended the main school in Watford.

The Wing was a windy, damp place, situated not far from the River Colne. My memories of starting secondary school are of the rain pouring down the Wing's windows, forcing us to stay inside at recreation times, competing for places to sit on the fat hot-water pipes. I reached the Wing normally by bike, but if the weather was bad, I took the train from Carpenders Park to Watford High Street station and walked up the High Street and then turned right into the aptly-named Water Lane. From here there was about a mile's walk to the Wing, passing over the Colne, which had a tendency to flood its banks, so the pavement had been pragmatically raised on stilts to allow people to traverse the flood. There was just no way to stop kids from going to school in the fifties.

Our form master was Mr. William Spouge, an English language teacher who was about twenty-eight years old. Spouge was a plump individual with thinning black, curly hair. He was not actually often with us – in fact only for English and French lessons, but he was our man. He was quite dedicated to getting Hertfordshire boys to sound their consonants (try not be 'swede bashers' he would say) and to grasp the rudiments of the English language. Spouge was one of the better teachers – many were probably ex-servicemen, de-mobbed from the Second World War with some basic teaching skills, but few of them were seriously deep into education as a vocation.

In our first year we studied English (mostly grammar, but little literature), history (this is a Roman arch, this is a Norman arch etc.), mathematics (we could already do fractions and decimals so logarithms were the new torture), geography (only England), music (get out your recorders boys), art (linocuts etc.), woodwork, RE (Religious Education), PE (Physical Education), games (football or cross country running in the winter, cricket or cross country running in the summer) and French (we struggled through the verbs *etre* and *avoir*).

I quite liked English, maths, PE, games (football and cricket, please), music (I had private piano lessons so for me it was basic stuff at school) and French, but art, woodwork, history, RE, and geography were boring. So, let's talk about the subjects that I didn't like.

The art class was given by Mr. Bernard Church, a tall, bearded man who just expected you to have artistic talent, or not. No way was he going to try and bring out some creativity in you. Church had a short fuse and would not tolerate any misbehaviour from us in class. I mean none at all, no laughing or even smiling. For him art was a serious business. And woe betide you if you didn't go along with this. Church possessed the biggest pair of feet I have ever seen, and kept a size thirteen crepe-soled sandal to administer his justice. How many times did my old friend from Carpenders Park, Colin Heathcote, get Church's wrath going? Colin was either fearless or was going through an early stupid phase. At almost every lesson, it would be, "Heathcote, stop slopping paint over Lombardi, and come out here to the front of the class."

The slipper was brought out of its cupboard and then, "Grasp both ankles, Heathcote," and blam, a terrible whack on the bum was administered. Most kids cried, but Colin was made of strong stuff. He never gave Church the chance to see him tearful. I noticed after about ten slipperings, Colin perfected the art of quickly standing up as the slipper was brought down, a sort of follow-through movement which must have lessened the impact. In this fractious atmosphere, it is not surprising my own artistic efforts were minimal. I just wanted the lessons to end.

I remember one boy in our class, David Broom, a thin, dark-haired, quiet lad, who was quite good at art. He would sidle over to my mess of a distant view of hills taken through a pair of binoculars, and say, "Oh, that's good, much better than mine."

And then you would see he had produced something Michelangelo would have been proud of.

Corporal punishment was only banned in schools in the 1980s and at Victoria Boys' school it took the form of canings or slipperings. It was used frequently for first- and second-year boys but, by the time I was fourteen, it had almost stopped. The head master, Mr. T. Price, administered the cane to boys who had seriously offended. His deputy was Mr. J. Hard, a mild-mannered man, who you had to be careful of as he caned quickly for minor offences. There were some tough, difficult kids at Victoria, who were always fighting and bullying other kids so in accordance with the customs of those times, corporal punishment did not seem out of place. I only had the slipper once from Mr. Fred Downs, and the cane once from Mr. Price for being caught card gambling for pennies. Kids like my friend Colin Heathcote seemed to not care at all about the punishments – I think it was an early form of machismo. Later in my life I was very glad to see corporal punishment banned in schools.

Mr. Jock Chalmers was our woodwork master, a dour Scot, who, it was rumoured, had lost a leg. I always wondered if his false leg was actually made of wood and he had made it himself, in the evenings after classes. I could just imagine him toiling away thinking, "Nearly finished and at least I don't have to pay for this".

On our introduction to woodwork classes, Chalmers assembled the whole class of twelve-year-old boys around a couple of benches in the woodwork shops which lined the end of the playground of the main school in Watford. Very sensibly he then gave us a lecture on the dangers of using saws, hammers, chisels, and screwdrivers. He demonstrated the errors he had seen made by boys in the past and one still sticks in my mind, being the wrong use of a pencil compass. He took out a brass compass used for drawing circles and showed how, if you used it as just a pencil by turning its point straight in line with the pencil, when you bent down to see better, you could easily stick the sharpened point into your eyeball. Later when we were struggling to produce our fruit bowls from solid pieces of walnut, it was, of course, Heathcote who was caught out trying to clamp the back of someone's overall into a vice. Chalmers arraigned Colin in front of the class.

"Stop work now, everybody. This silly idiot," slap around head, "thinks he's being clever," slap around head again. "Detention after school for one hour and write out one hundred lines of *I must not use tools incorrectly in woodwork classes.*"

Poor Colin, he was only bored, I suppose, like us all.

My younger brother, Victor, remembers seeing Chalmers on TV much later in life when he was one of the first patients to receive a ground-breaking new hip replacement. Vic remembers Chalmers speaking to the camera telling the audience how difficult it had been for him to move about and what pain he had been in, but then he started jumping up and down, jogging on the spot and saying, "But noo I ken jump and skip." So, he didn't actually have a wooden leg – it was just a Victorian legend.

History, which I realised later in life is essential to understanding the time you are living in by giving you an appreciation of what has come before, was restricted to learning about medieval times and the conquests of Britain. Now, with the fantastic BBC4 television programmes, I am captured by the history of ancient civilizations and have learnt so much from stories told by great presenters. Past times, depicted in indecipherable languages inscribed in stone, can show us insights of the values and lives of people from three thousand years ago. However, this never happened at Victoria with Mr. Crowsher. He finally became the permanent history teacher, following the three stand-in history masters we had in my first year, and they all repeated what the last one had told us. "This is a Roman arch, this is a Norman arch…" Sigh.

Raymond Gunstone was a large man of about thirty. He looked like he should have been playing rugby for England. He was mild-mannered, polite and on a mission from God to get some religious education into the thick heads of Victoria's schoolboys. My mother went to church regularly, erring I like to think on the safe side, so consequently Steve and I had been brought up to go to Sunday School from the age of six. Later on, I went with her to the Methodist Church at South Oxhey every Sunday evening, so I was already familiar with the New Testament and most of the important stories and characters from the Old Testament.

'Gunner' Gunstone however, went through it all again by having boys read passages from the Bible in class. Thank goodness the lessons were only for one hour a week. He noticed I had a good speaking voice and was able to read the Bible easily, even if I had not read the passage previously. Victoria Secondary Modern Boys' School started every school day with an assembly of the whole school. The head master led the assembly which began with a Bible reading by a boy who was selected by Gunner, then a hymn and a prayer, and finally, announcements. Somehow, the boys often failed to turn up, so Gunner was left flapping around at the last minute to find someone else to do it. Once I was in the second year, he used me whenever he could as a stand-in. I didn't mind, it gave me the chance to look out from the raised stage over hundreds of boys and watch them surreptitiously mucking about. Gunner, in my opinion had completely missed his vocation – he should have been a sports master. With his keenness and friendly manner, he could have been an inspiration to boys but, unfortunately, as an RE teacher, he failed in his mission.

Our geography lessons seemed to revolve around drawing maps of Great Britain, which is difficult enough, I mean it's not boot-shaped like Italy, is it? And then colouring in regions like the Broads, the Lake District, or Wales. Fascinating stuff. I think Mr. F. Tipler was our master for this subject, who seemed as bored with the curriculum as we were.

In 1957, nearly all the boys in our class wore short trousers. The school uniform was obligatory and consisted of grey trousers, white shirt, school tie, navy blue blazer and cap. My mum relented and let me wear long trousers when I was thirteen, but I had to go through the winter of 1957-58 up to my birthday in February in short ones.

Imagine doing that in the freezing rain, riding three miles each way to school and back, twice a day. I went home for dinner, I just could not stomach the school food. On my first day at Victoria Main School, my mum sensibly decided that, like Steve, I would stay for the school lunch and I sat down at a trestle table erected in the main hall, which also doubled as a gymnasium. I remember the meal, a sort of stew with potatoes served from stainless steel containers in which the meal had just been delivered – there were no kitchen facilities in the school – and which was ladled out by large ladies in pink aprons. The smell had already more or less deterred my appetite, but I tried the meat which I found disgusting, so I then tried eating some black-eyed potatoes but eventually gave up and surveyed the dessert – semolina with a blob of jam in it. One of the boys, David Pomfret I think, said, "Oh, this semolina smells a bit off," and when I stupidly bent my head down to smell it, someone rammed my head into my plate. I was forced to retire swiftly to the toilets to clean myself up.

At the New Wing, where there were no shops, only rows of houses around the school, after trying the meals I found them to be just as bad as those at the main school. My mum gave me the five shillings which the school meals cost every week and let me decide if I wanted to come home, or buy something to eat in the town where I would go with other boys to buy some chips and a bread and butter roll. But normally I rode home by bike to an empty house (my mum was at work), and made myself a soup or an egg on toast.

In the second year at Victoria our form master was 'Gunner' Gunstone, and we were only at the Wing for metalwork classes one morning a week. The subjects were the same as the previous year, but in maths we started to do some basic algebra and geometry. Music lessons were led by Mr. Nigel Sagar, a slender, intense man about thirty years old. Sagar had his own music classroom complete with grand piano. We were given recorders to play, which belonged to the school, and the rigmarole of their sterilisation is my strongest memory. A tin pail full of disinfectant was placed in the front of the class. You had to dip the mouthpiece of your recorder into the fluid and then shake it dry into the bucket. The smell was as ghastly as the taste. No wonder none of us seemed to be keen on these lessons.

Once Sagar understood I could read music, he asked me to stay behind and play something for him. I was never an inspired music student and only played piano to please my mother, practising one hour religiously every night. I was at about Grade 4, I suppose, and hadn't realised that I had a poor sense of time, but I did have an excellent memory for the musical score. I played Sagar whatever it was I was practising with Mr. Graves, and needed no music to do it. Sagar didn't say much, but immediately pressed me into the school band.

Steve was already playing trumpet in the band, and Sagar said they needed someone to play the trombone – it was easy, he convinced me. I stayed behind one evening a week with this big trombone. With Steve's help, I got the hang of blowing the notes quite quickly, but the slide was the real problem. I was twelve years old and probably one of the smallest kids in the class. My big problem was when you needed to play a note which required the trombone slide to be fully extended, my arm was not long enough to play the note and then get the slide back. I finally solved the problem by bending forward and letting the slide fall out of my reach, blowing the note and then flicking myself backwards to catch the slide so I could continue playing other notes again. Not a great success and I am glad to say it did not last long before a tall boy from another class, who was in the Salvation Army, took over.

Sagar was an accomplished musician, but slightly big-headed. One time sitting at his grand piano, he said to the class, "When Bartok wrote his first piano concerto there were only two men in the world who could actually play it."

And then he gave a little, "Hmm Hmm," and launched into the piece, bending his head furiously over the keys, his hands flying all over the key board. I suppose he must have been the third...

But Sagar was alright. He had a record player in his music room and played us lots of classical pieces and tried to explain their merits. On rare occasions, he also played us some jazz and tried to show us the difference between traditional and modern jazz. My strongest memory is of him playing us a record of the song *Strange Fruit* by Billie Holiday. He explained that the song depicted the bodies of black men who had been hanged from the limbs of trees by racist white fanatics in the southern states of the USA. The haunting tone of her voice rang about the Victorian plaster ceiling of the classroom and beckoned to another world across the sea, where jazz was a part of people's sad lives. At the end of our second year the school held a traditional jazz concert with parts of the school band from Steve's class playing saxophone, tea chest bass, and drums, with Nigel Sagar on piano. The school assembly hall rocked for the first time in its history.

Games were held for a full afternoon each week in Cassiobury Park, the school having no sports ground of its own. We used to assemble in the school playground at 1.30pm with our kit, such as football shorts, shirts and boots which we carried in our satchels and then we would walk there with the games teacher.

Cassiobury Park is one of the best things about Watford. It is a large formal park which would take at least an hour to walk around. There were some changing rooms and cold (only) showers about halfway down the park. There were probably six football pitches set amongst the wonderful ancient horse chestnut and oak trees. Mr. Fred Downs, a young teacher of about twenty-five years old, was our games master for our first year, and I honestly don't think he knew the rules of football very well. I had to explain the offside rule to him several times after he had blatantly let some goal-hanging kid score a goal, when he was completely offside. He was also incredibly short-sighted.

Most of the children at Vics, as the school was familiarly called, came from Watford's primary schools. However, my primary school was called St. Meryl and although it was within the Watford rural area, it was three miles away at Carpenders Park, almost in Middlesex. Most of the other boys came from primary schools like Watford Fields, Chater, or Beecham Grove and others.

Early in our first year, the new Victoria First Year Football Eleven was invited to go back to Watford Fields, the old school of my classmates 'Bugs' Martindale and

Peter Hancock, to play a game against their first team, who were of course a year younger than us. Now, you will remember one year at twelve years old is almost an eternity, so they should have been easy opposition for us. But no, for there in the shade of Benskin's Brewery, by half-time they were already up two nil. Having been elected captain I decided at this moment to remove our 'Foxy' Fowler from his position as goalkeeper, where he claimed to have played for his primary school, and replace him with Cliff Langley, who was a tall lad for his age and in my class. I had noticed in the playground Cliff had safe hands. I also swopped 'Bugs' Martindale to the inside forward position to partner Melvyn Bailey and moved Bobby Keeler to left half. Keeler had a strange ambling gait that fooled many defenders and by the final whistle we had won 5 – 2, Peter Hancock having scored two goals zooming in from right wing.

Our games against other schools did not fare so well, especially when we played at home with Fred Downs as the home referee. We generally did better when playing away, often beating our greatest rivals Leggatts Way School, and also Bushey Meads, Langlebury, Clarendon, and Hampden. However, we could never beat the Catholic school from North Watford, St Michael's. Not in the five years I played football for Victoria. In our second year a young guy named Melvyn Brisbane joined the school and played for the School Eleven. Melvyn had a natural football talent and was far above the standard of anyone else. He eventually made a professional career playing for Watford FC. He raised our game enormously. He had a wonderful left foot and could kick the ball very hard. Sometimes we played home matches at the Wing where there was a sloping pitch, and time and again, we would kick off facing down the pitch and Melvyn would receive the ball from the centre forward and shoot from the halfway line, completely lobbing the goalkeeper, who could only look astounded as the ball sailed over his head into the goal net. 1 – 0 already. How we would grin.

However, football does depend a lot on your physique and fitness, and I noticed as boys grew older, they either got better or worse. Some of the original First Eleven just never grew enough or lost interest perhaps and slipped out of the team. They were replaced by kids who had either improved their skills or grown physically to be better. Colin Heathcote and I were always about the same size between the ages of eight to thirteen years, and then he started to grow faster than me. Colin grew steadily to reach six foot by the time he was eighteen and by then his football had improved so much he was playing for Herts County at the weekends. During my fourth year the School Eleven had a football match against the Masters Eleven, they were surprisingly good at first, but then faded quickly – we beat them 3 – 0.

Mr. Michael Crump was a young teacher who joined Victoria in 1957. It was his first teaching post. He was often responsible for organising our sports afternoons. Soon we discovered someone was stealing personal possessions from our changing-rooms in Cassiobury Park, while we were absent on the pitches. Crump decided to catch the thief and hid himself in the changing rooms after we had left to play football. He caught the thief red-handed and gave chase when he fled. The man didn't realise Michael

Crump was fit, a fast sprinter and only twenty-two years old. He was quickly overtaken and apprehended. There were no more thefts after that.

Recreation breaks at school were held halfway through the morning and afternoon. In the morning-break free school milk was offered in one-third pint bottles. Unfortunately, in the winter it was often frozen solid. The main occupation for me and my friends during these periods was playing football using a tennis ball in the school yard. I passed many hours with Peter Hancock, Colin Heathcote, 'Bugs' Martindale, Melvyn Bailey, Cliff Langley, David Elson, and Peter ('Bomber') Lombardi kicking a tennis ball around the tarmac. Other pastimes for those less inclined were French Cricket, 'fag' cards, and of course the joys of the Tuck Shop. The Tuck Shop was manned by a boy in his fifth year and sold Pepsi Cola, Fanta and biscuits. You could buy single biscuits for one penny each. You were not allowed out of school during recreation, the massive, old, blue metal gates remained firmly closed.

School began at 9am and you normally had to be inside the gates by 8.55am. Prefects manned the gates and if you were late your name was marked into a book and you usually received detention, unless you had a valid reason. So, generally, I arrived at least fifteen minutes before nine o'clock, and was almost never late. I think I was ill and absent for only one day in my five years at Victoria.

During my brother Steve's second year, before I arrived, a photo was taken of the complete school. There were so many boys in the photo it needed a frame about a metre long and was one of his prized possessions. I often wondered during my time at Vics, when they would repeat the photo, but it never happened. Well, actually it did. In my last year after taking GCE 'O' levels, on a fine day in late June, Colin Heathcote and I took the day off, as a sort of reward for all the study we had done. Classes were finished and there were only two weeks left of our time at Victoria, so attendance for us was quite relaxed. We spent a great day at Bushey open-air swimming pool, only to be told by Peter Hancock the next day a photo had been taken of the complete school. I never mentioned it to my mum, who only asked me once why no photo had ever been taken. I could hardly have bought it and not appeared in it. But it was a bit ironic, since my attendance during five years was almost perfect…

Lunchtime was at 12pm and lasted until 1.30pm. You were free to leave the school or stay for school dinners. On the corner of the alley which led to the boys' school was a sweet shop offering all the normal delights like Ha'penny Chews, Black Jacks, Sherbet Lemons, Arrowroot sticks, and in the summer the wonderful frozen Jubblies, which were triangular prisms of frozen orange juice. A beaten-up bubble-gum dispenser was set into the pavement outside the shop displaying its brightly-coloured gum balls, which could be bought by inserting a penny.

By the time I was in the third year at Vics I could afford to buy a good bicycle with my savings from my paper and grocery rounds. I bought a British racing bike, an A. S. Gillott for fifteen pounds on which I could cycle the three miles from home to school easily in fifteen minutes. When school finished at 4pm I was normally home by 4.20pm at the latest. However, it was out of the question to keep the bike at school during the day, it would have been stripped immediately. So luckily for me Peter Hancock, who lived nearby in St. Mary's Road, allowed me to leave it safely in his back-garden. He became my closest friend at school and we sat next to one another whenever we could.

Physical education was held twice a week either inside, in the main assembly hall lined on each side with wooden wall bars, or outside in the playground. All the gym classes were managed by the same teacher, Mr. Peter Tomblin. 'Tombo' was good-looking, thirtyish, drove a sleek white Ford car, and was slim and fit. He was also hopelessly narcissistic and seemed to be permanently tanned and searching for dark windows to look into. It was Peter Hancock, who had many older, worldly-wise sisters, who explained the tan came out of a bottle. I was amazed.

'Tombo' organised us into Victoria's house colours, which were named after the four rivers of Watford: Colne (red), Gade (blue), Chess (yellow) and Ver (green). I was in Chess. The gym classes in the hall varied, but we used quite a lot of equipment like leather bucks and horses to jump over, and wall bars for stretching and climbing. 'Tombo' always got us to compete in our house teams. Poor Arthur Lythaby in Gade was the only overweight boy in the class and these PE lessons were torture for him. 'Tombo' would help Arthur to ascend the buck and watch him struggle with insufficient arm muscle to propel himself over it. The rest of us were pretty thin, having been brought up on rationing after the Second World War, when food was still in short supply. There was almost nobody in my class who came from a middle-class background, we were all working-class at Victoria.

Outside in the playground we would play games in our house teams like skittle-ball, where two big skittles were placed inside painted rings on the tarmac, and each team had to defend their own and attack the other's, trying to knock it over with a ball. These PE lessons lasted an hour and I enjoyed them a lot. It taught you about team play and fairness. I think it also provided young boys with the chance to let off steam and get rid of some energy. Tomblin had his own classroom on the side of the school which faced the girls' school. All the classrooms on this side had sash windows glazed with frosted glass so you could not see out or in. They were protected on the far side by chain-link netting, so when the girls played netball, the windows would not be broken. In the summer when not taking a PE class, 'Tombo' always had the window next to his desk slightly open so he could watch the girls play in their shorts.

French was a subject which intrigued me. At twelve years old, it seemed like a code you could speak and no-one else would know what you were saying. I thought by having mastered the verbs *etre* (to be) and *avoir* (to have) all you needed to do was learn lots of nouns and you would be speaking French. We struggled through *etre* and *avoir* with William Spouge in our first year, and after about four lessons he produced a small book '*Pierre et les Cambrioleurs*', a short story about Peter and the robbers. I do not actually remember finishing the book, so I don't know if the robbers got caught or not.

In our second year a new master arrived at the school, Mr. T. Alford, who became our master for French. Terry Alford had moved out of London from teaching at a rough school in Cricklewood and when he first started at Victoria, he was so hard and tough, not tolerating any misbehaviour and quickly shouting at us, we all felt terrorized. He settled down after a bit, when he realised Vics was not in a war zone. I remember he used to pass me in the corridor and he'd say "*Salut Salaud*", which later when I lived in France, I discovered means, "Greetings you bastard", loosely translated. In our third year, we had Mr. Langham, who insisted we speak French throughout the lesson. He would stand in front of the class, grasping the lapels of his jacket with both hands while teaching. Langham decided we would all adopt French names. I wanted Henri, but someone else got it before me, so I had to settle for Thomas. I was never happy with this.

When our third year began, we were surprised to see a whole new addition to Victoria in the form of numerous, mostly red-haired, Scottish lads. These were boys from the Royal Caledonian School in Bushey, who were poor children of Scottish parents. They only boarded at their school but travelled to local schools to attend classes, and due to an increase in their numbers it became Victoria's turn to educate them. Jock Maclean joined us in Form 3 and became quite a useful centre half in the 3rd Eleven. The 'Callies', as they were known, were dressed in grey uniforms and initially wore kilts. No wonder they were involved in lots of playground fights.

In the fifties and sixties, the Watford area had three Grammar schools which provided the means to study for higher education. The Secondary schools, such as Victoria, provided boys with a technical education specializing in trade classes of woodwork, metalwork and technical drawing, aiming to get boys into craft apprenticeships.

The leaving age was fifteen years old. There were several big printing companies in Watford, founded on the four rivers which ran through the town, which, coupled with the paper industry at Croxley, provided the opportunity for boys from Victoria to most likely find a job in the printing industry.

Watford also had a Technical school which provided the opportunity of taking GCE 'O' and 'A' levels as a portal to a future technical career. Steve, Victor and I were very fortunate that Victoria also provided, at fifteen years old, the possibility for the top stream to stay on an extra year to take subjects at GCE 'O' level. Not many other secondary modern schools in Watford offered this opportunity. Victoria's top class was prepared for this at fourteen, when boys were in their third year. Potential GCE students were placed in a class called 5 Lower for their fourth year. The fifth year, at sixteen, was called 5 Upper. Consequently, learning became a lot more serious at fourteen, history was dropped from the curriculum and I was introduced to two teachers who were to have a big influence on my school life.

Cyril Fenton was our form master during our third year and was also the best English teacher in the school. Cyril was a kindly, white-haired man in his late forties. He dressed well, had charisma and as we had been selected to take GCE 'O' levels, he tried to make us feel special. He eventually left teaching and became Mayor of Rickmansworth, a neighbouring smaller town. Cyril loved the English language and did his level best to pass that love on to us. In his year we were introduced to English literature and read *The Autobiography of a Super Tramp* by W. H. Davies, the real life adventures of a man who decided to become a tramp in the USA; *Jennie* by Paul Gallico, a fantasy story of a boy who has an accident and while he is unconscious, fighting for his life, dreams he is a cat and enters the feline world and experiences all of its precariousness; and *A Pattern of Islands* by Sir Arthur Grimble, a funny and charming story of the life of a young British administrator in the Pacific Islands of Gilbert and Ellis. Cyril also plunged us into the more complicated side of English grammar and started teaching us parsing, the analysis of sentences into their constituent parts, e.g. clauses and phrases.

For mathematics, we were introduced to Mr. Jack Spours, a talented teacher who was also the senior sports master in the school. Mr. Spours had a 'no nonsense' approach to maths and being a tall, dark-haired man with a serious and rather over-bearing manner, he put the fear of God into the class. His strong North Country voice would ring out and hammer home mathematic principles, with which he seemed to have a personal affinity. If you didn't understand it, Spours took it seriously (and personally) and had you behind after the class to see where in your dense head he had gone wrong. He actually had a logical way of teaching maths and if you paid attention and did your homework, normally all went well and you progressed. If you did not understand, one of Spours's favourite sayings was, 'Look to the Book', which to us Watford lads sounded just like, 'Luuk to the Buuk'. We were introduced to algebra in detail, first to simple equations, then simultaneous equations and finally quadratic equations. He also taught us the first thirty theorems of geometry, which are alright for the first twenty or so, but then become quite complicated, especially as you have to prove them each time. We also continued trigonometry, venturing into higher ordered functions.

In 5 Lower our form master was Mr. Ron Atkinson, the technical drawing master. French had been dropped, except for a few boys in the class who continued, and general science was with Mr. T. Heath. We were being prepared to take five subjects in the GCE 'O' level exams which were selected from: art, English, mathematics (arithmetic, algebra and trigonometry), general science (physics, chemistry and biology), geography and either metalwork or technical drawing. This was our curriculum for the last two years at school plus, of course, the mandatory PE and games. Music and woodwork were dropped. During the fourth year, 5 Lower still took the national leaving school exam for fifteen-year olds, which was called the Area Certificate, but in preparation for the GCE 'O' level we also took a more difficult national exam, The College of Preceptors Exam.

General science took place in a post-war building squeezed onto the Watford school site, which was called the Annex, containing the 5 Lower and 5 Upper classrooms, a science laboratory, the secretary's office and an art room. On its far side there was a boiler room for the school's heating system which was the home of Mr. Stacey, the school janitor, a man who seemed to be always dressed in blue overalls and had a perpetually lined face. I don't think life had been kind to him, as he definitely did not like boys much.

'Ted' Heath (after the band leader) was our science teacher, a small man with dark walnut skin and furtive brown eyes. The lab contained benches with centrally positioned gas taps. We attached Bunsen burners to these when making experiments. The boys loved to turn them on without lighting them, but in our first lesson Heath explained how dangerous this could be, and did we all want an explosion to carry us to Watford FC football pitch? Under his strict control we performed experiments like heating a beaker of water with potassium permanganate in it, then allowing it to cool and evaporate to observe the formation of purplish-black crystals. I found science interesting, but there was insufficient time to ask questions. Biology was fine and chemistry was okay, but physics was more difficult. I never completely understood how you solved chemical transformation equations. Also, I think the main problem was in maths, an equation uses known precepts to solve it, but in chemistry you seemed to need to know the solution already. I guess the rules were not properly explained.

Metalwork classes took place at the Wing. I only did them for one year with Mr. Pereira, who once again went to great lengths to try to stop boys from hurting themselves with the potentially dangerous tools. First, we made a picture hook which was cut out of a brass sheet and shaped into a trapezium and then bent so it could hook onto the picture-rail at one end and a picture frame at the other. I found one of these in a box in my mum's house when she moved into a care home in 2009. I think my younger brother Victor had made it about fifty years earlier. We also made a fire poker out of a length of quarter-inch square steel bar, sharpened at one end and turned into a closed circle at the other. The poker was twisted at its centre length, giving us experience in using the forge to heat up the metal and becoming used to hammering the hot steel into shapes. It was when Lombardi was giving his one a final polishing, by applying it to a greased, leather, buffing wheel, it became hot, due to friction. Lombardi tried holding the metal poker with his overall strap, but it got caught in the buffing wheel and would have pulled him into the machine if he had not managed to press the red STOP button in time. Then of course we were lectured with, "This silly idiot…," clip around ear, etc. Some boys loved using the metalwork tools and machines, but not me.

Every spring, we all had to take part in a cross-country race of about three miles in Cassiobury Park. This race was always organised by Jack Spours and he would not permit anyone to miss it. It normally rained. Before the race Spours would have all the boys lined up in front of him in the school yard, to explain the course. It was the same every year, reasonably easy, apart from a stiff climb about halfway through called Jacotts Hill. The first part was through the park to the river Gade and then he got to, "Over the bridge down to the woodcutter's hut. Up Jacotts," and here he would smile wickedly, this being the difficult bit and he would post a teacher there to be sure no-one skived off. In our class was a thin, quiet, tallish guy named Ian Brooks, who was a member of the Watford Harriers sports club. Brooks would far outpace everyone else and win every time. During my fifth year I did some training with him and grew to like running too.

The last year at Victoria was definitely the best. We were the oldest boys in the school, aloof and apart, our classroom on the top floor of the Annex. Study became a big part of my life, as it would be for many years afterwards. We took mock GCE Oxford version 'O' level papers, however, you never knew if they would ask a question on something Victoria had not covered. Not everybody took all the subjects. I took maths, English, geography, general science and technical drawing and a further subject called Certificate of Proficiency in Arithmetic. I think these were quite difficult exams for children of sixteen years old. The level was quite high, so when you were looking for a job afterwards, they were an excellent benchmark for employers, or for screening entrance into a grammar school to continue full-time education to 'A' levels. I passed all my subjects and managed to find a job in engineering, which I studied part-time until I was twenty-three, eventually qualifying as a Chartered Structural Engineer at twenty-five years old.

So, the worst school in Watford did me proud. With the help of more experienced teachers, like Jack Spours and Cyril Fenton, I discovered if I persevered, I could succeed. My brother Steve did an apprenticeship in production engineering, immigrated to Australia, embraced the computerization of his industry, and became a published specialist in his field of flow-manufacturing and vice-president of an American management consultancy.

My younger brother Victor started at Victoria six years after me in 1962 and a little later the school leaving age was increased to sixteen years old. This had an enormous effect on many schools with existing establishments having to find place for about twenty percent more students. For Victoria this was impossible, so a new school was built and opened in Tolpits Lane, complete with swimming pool and state-of-the-art woodwork and metalwork shops. Victor passed his 'O' levels, and went on to study full-time for a Higher National Diploma in Business Studies at Watford Technical College and started his own successful business, which flourishes strongly today.

Of all the teachers mentioned here I only know that Michael Crump is still alive today, but I would like to thank them all anyway, for their help and also just for being a part of my early life.

Wolf Cubs and Boy Scouts

When I was a little kid, the best night of the week was Friday, when my brother Steve and I went to Wolf Cubs in Oxhey, the next stop from Carpenders Park on the Bakerloo line going towards Watford.

The Wolf Cubs in the UK were for boys from the age of eight to ten years old. After this period, you graduated to the Boy Scouts. Our Cub and Scout groups were called the 29th South West Herts, and were associated and supported by the Oxhey Methodist Church. This was a Victorian sandstone brick building of rather massive proportions which was built in 1905. It occupied the corner of King Edward's Road and Chalk Hill, the road leading up to Bushey. I'd attended this church's Sunday School from the age of five years old until I was nearly eight, sitting in a little chair in what was originally called the Galahad Room, learning about the Bible. Our stepfather used to work nights at the Sun Printers in Watford and I think my parents needed to get rid of my brother and me on Sunday afternoons, so they could have some time for a nap in bed after Sunday lunch. We duly collected the nice books the church presented us with each year for achieving one hundred percent attendance. I still remember my favourite, *The Ghostly Galleon,* by Admiral Lord Mountevans.

But all this early religious instruction stopped once my mum realised Steve and I had begun to play 'hooky' and instead of going to Sunday School, we went to Oxhey Park fishing for tiddlers with a jam jar. So, she enrolled us in the Cubs instead, where we could learn something practical and interesting.

I remember joining Steve, who had started going to Cubs before me, on my 8th birthday in February and not being allowed to wear the uniform until I had passed my tenderfoot tests. This took about two weeks and then my mum bought me the green jersey, green cap and yellow neckerchief, these being the colours for the 29th SW Herts Scout troop. The neckerchief was worn with the essential 'woggle', a small, woven, leather ring-like contraption which held the scarf tight around your neck. I felt great in the uniform and my mum sewed on the badge for the Pack's notation.

Once a month on Sunday morning, the Cubs would join the Scouts for Church Parade. We lined up in King Edward's Road behind the Scout group and then with our 29th SW Herts flag flying in the breeze, we would follow the flag bearer and march into the church, swelling the congregation with our numbers. We Cubs felt proud in our uniforms, and I have to say our green peaked caps with their yellow braiding were actually quite snazzy. The khaki short trousers, however, could not mask our knobbly little knees.

The Cub Pack leaders organised all sorts of games for kids from eight to ten years, as a pre-training for the Boy Scouts. There was much competitive play and also some sensible training, mixed in with understanding discipline and getting a sense of community living. At times, the play was a bit rough, which I liked, and both Steve and I often came out on top – so we got some credibility from our Cub peers.

The Cubs' meetings were from 7.30 to 8.30pm on Friday evenings. The Cub Pack was led by a kind man who we called Akela, who was assisted by a young man called Baloo. Both these names are used in Cub language, inspired by the books of Rudyard Kipling. The evening started with all the Cubs, organised into teams of six boys known as Sixes, forming a horseshoe shape around Akela and Baloo. This was known as the Grand Howl and when Akela explained what we would be doing during the evening. Then the Howl was closed by the 'Senior Sixer' holding up a four-foot high pole topped by a remarkably good plaster effigy of a wolf's head, shouting, "Well, DYB DYB DYB," and all the pack would respond with, "Well, DOB DOB DOB." This was a call to 'Do Your Best' and the response was, 'Do Our Best'. I found it a bit cryptic, but at the time we accepted it all as just part of being a Cub.

Each of the Cub's Sixes was led by a boy of ten years old who was called a sixer, who had an assistant called a second. Our sixes were named after a colour – I was in Blue. The evening was normally divided into different periods. We would be instructed how to progress through the Cub Programme by perfecting small tasks perhaps not all boys would learn at home, like how to make a telephone call from a public call box. In those times it was more complicated than making a call today. You lifted the receiver, put in your money and dialled the number. Then you waited until the call was connected and if someone answered, you pressed button A to connect to the party. If there was no answer, or you had dialled a wrong number or you just wanted to stop the call, you hung up and pressed button B to get your money back. Afterwards every time I saw a red telephone box, I opened the door and pressed button B to see if someone had forgotten to do this, in the hope I might get someone else's money back. Back to the Cub tasks – we also learnt how to tie basic knots and to identify common trees, bushes and wild animals.

We tried to do things at home to win badges for specified activities, such as collecting. I brought in my stamp album and this was reviewed by Baloo. He asked me questions about it and judged me to be a serious enough collector and awarded me my Collector's badge, which depicted a magnifying glass on a blue background. This was my first badge and it was presented to me in front of the pack at a Grand Howl. My mum sewed the triangular badge onto the top of my right sleeve, just down from the shoulder. When you had gained six badges you won a special activity award badge and were presented with a five-inch long sheath-knife. Nowadays, this would be rightly considered too dangerous to be given to young children. However, sixty years ago was a different time and Cubs were trusted not to abuse this honour. We were proud of our sheath-knives and they served us well during our service in the Boy Scouts too. Mine was bone-handled and had a companion smaller sheath knife attached on the front of the big sheath. I often wonder what happened to it. They were prize possessions when both Steve and I were young, but I expect my mother nursed a fear of them and quietly disposed of them when we left home.

The best part of the evening was when we played games like 'Hopping Sailors', where one boy was placed in the middle of the hall and the rest had to hop past him. With his arms folded across his chest he tried to knock you over by hopping and bumping into you. When someone was felled, he joined the boy in the middle and they both tried to topple more boys, until there was only one left for everyone to get.

I remember one evening when Akela threw a rope over one of the ceiling beams about five metres above the ground. He then fastened the free end and let the rope hang down. The boys had to try and climb up the rope. At eight to ten years old not many boys have strong arm muscles, so few of them could do it. The rest of the pack did not know how much time Steve and I spent climbing trees in the spinney behind our house, so when it was my turn, I shot straight up the rope and was about to climb onto the beam, when a surprised Akela called me to come down immediately. Still, I got a round of applause from the pack.

Baloo was a kind lad about sixteen years old, whose real name was Dave Garrett. When Steve went on to join the Scout troop, I would walk to the Cubs' meeting via Dave's house in Villier's Road, Oxhey to meet him. These houses were little terraced Victorian properties and I can remember his mum letting me stand by their blazing coke fire in the lounge, waiting for him to get ready and then he and I would go to the Cubs' evening together.

The Church's Community Centre, where the Cub activities took place, had bare boards on the floor and frosted glass windows set into corrugated sheet-metal clad walls. The exterior walls were painted a dark green colour and in fact the entrance part of this structure was the original church from the nineteenth century, which had been used before the Methodist Church was built. Then it was called the 'Tin Tabernacle' and had been first erected in Villiers Road, Oxhey and later transplanted onto land adjacent to the newly-built church. Here it was extended to be used as a Sunday School and Church Community Centre.

The Wolf Cub evenings would end with a closing Grand Howl and we would gather our coats and head for the train station and home via the Villiers Road chip shop. Here we had threepenny servings of chips – wonderful hot fried potato chips laced with vinegar and sprinkled with salt. If, by some incredible fortune you had more money, then this treat could be topped off with a bottle of Tizer.

There were several other boys from Carpenders Park who were also in the Cubs, like Ken and Derek Clarke. We took the train home together, walking up the dark streets which were lined with woods near the station. Sometimes we dared to go via the 'short cut', through a spinney between the station exit and our road, St. George's Drive. It was pitch black in the woods which was quite frightening and just as we were nearly out of the dark trees someone would shout, "Here comes the bogey man!" and we would all race across the open field to the safety of the lights of St. George's Drive.

Akela and Baloo decided just after I joined the Cubs to take the pack on a weekend one-night camp to Bovingdon, a country area about eight miles away. All went well initially, with us Cubs helping to put up the tents and lay out our ground sheets. You have to remember this was 1953, so there were no sleeping bags, just grey blankets folded into beds held together with big blanket pins. Unfortunately, the weather quickly deteriorated into a big summer rain storm and we were completely washed out. All the Cubs were transferred with their soggy blankets to the farmer's barn where we spent the night tucked up in the hay. As the rain did not stop on the Sunday we remained in the barn and our parents were contacted to come and collect us early. It was a shame, but it didn't put me off camping.

St. George is the patron saint of the Scout Movement and every year, on the closest Sunday to St. George's Day, 23rd April, the Cubs and Scouts of the 29th SW Herts would march from the church in Oxhey up Watford High Street to the town hall. Here we would join other troops in celebrating the event.

One year I was asked to be the flag bearer for the Cubs and after the march from Oxhey to Watford I was positioned in the town hall, along with about twenty other flag bearers, behind all the dignitaries leading the celebration. The flags were propped against the wall behind us. Unfortunately, this particular year it was unseasonably hot, and the big town hall was completely packed out. I lasted nearly to the end of the ceremony, but then, feeling the effects of the heat and lack of air, I fainted, knocking over my flag, which in turn knocked over several others. I was carried outside and woke up breathing in smelling salts.

When I became a Boy Scout, I had to change my uniform to beige short trousers, beige short-sleeved shirt, yellow neckerchief with the woggle and a green beret. In the Scout troop, we were organised into 'Patrols' which were named after birds. There were the Swifts, the Curlews, the Kestrels and the Owls. Steve became Patrol Leader of the Curlews, so when I joined the Scouts I was placed in his patrol, where eventually I would become his Second.

The troop was led by Panther, a big strong man of twenty-eight years old, whose real name was Harry Hart. It took some authority to control twenty-four young boys who were between the ages of eleven to sixteen, but Harry was well up to the job. He was assisted by two younger men, Fleet and Doc, who were Panther's assistants. Doc was not a doctor, but he did have round glasses and was studying to go to university. The Scout hut was a dedicated building just next to the community centre, so all the Scout paraphernalia could be permanently left in there, unlike the Cubs who had to clear everything away into cupboards at the end of the evening, in order to let the building be used for jumble sales, amateur dramatics, dancing classes, etc.

The Scout hut was a rather rude affair, being constructed of light steel profiles and clad with asbestos sheeting. I am sure it disappeared sometime in the early sixties, when it became evident that asbestos was such a hazard to people's health. But in the fifties, we were all innocent of such things and I remember it with affection. It was not centrally heated like the community centre but had a couple of gas fires set into the walls, which were lit on cold, winter evenings. Each patrol was given a corner of the hut to be their area, and Panther and his lads would occupy a centre part of a side wall next to one of the fires.

In the fifties Scouts progressed through three classes: Tenderfoot stage, Second Class and then First Class. Each stage was reached by completing defined tests like map reading, use of a compass and the use of different knots, etc. These phases were quite detailed, with about twenty subjects to become proficient in. The Tenderfoot stage took about four weeks. However, the Second Class Certificate took about two years, so you were about thirteen years old when you got it. The First Class Certificate took about the same time, so at the age of fifteen years old you could be a First Class Boy Scout. Each stage required you to spend a minimum number of nights under canvas (i.e. camping) and for the First Class you had to make a two-day hike, accompanied by just one other scout, and then present your experience written up into a log.

I accompanied a Scout who was taking his First Class Hike in the White Horse Hills of Wiltshire. We were given instructions in the form of map coordinates to follow, making the fifteen-mile hike between these references, and had to note all we saw to prove we had been there. We knew we had followed the hike correctly, for at the last map reference, we found we were standing on the eye of the White Horse. We had a glorious two days tramping about the Wiltshire countryside, putting up our tent on the hills and cooking sausages. I made my own First Class Hike when I was Patrol Leader of the Curlews, accompanied by Alan 'Muscles' Cross, Patrol Leader of the Owls. It was closer to home, starting in Redbourne Village, eventually passing through Whippendale Woods and ending up in Cassiobury Park in Watford.

The 29th SW Herts went on a summer camp in the school holidays to the Isle of Wight, on a farm near Blackgang Chine, about six miles from Ventnor. The beaches were a bit dangerous, surrounded by steep ravine-like cliffs of crumbling clay which were eroding fast. This area is near to the southern tip of the island and is not a great bathing place – in fact it has a long history of smuggling. We were allowed to use a farmer's field to pitch our tents, about two miles back from the Chine. Each patrol had its own tent and we were inspected every day after breakfast. Patrols drew their rations from the Stores and were responsible for cooking their own food, washing up after meals and keeping their tent and area clean. There were enormous differences in levels, depending on the diligence of the Patrol Leaders. The Curlews were led by Steve and tried to be the best patrol. Our main competition were the Swifts, led by Peter Hardwick and his brother Martin, who was his second. The Owls tried a bit but actually had rather low standards, and the Kestrels, to which my friend Colin Heathcote belonged, just seemed to muck about all the time.

Sometimes we played 'Wide Games' which were organised by Panther with the troop divided into two groups, one of which had to defend a designated area against the other. You were given a 'life', which was a strand of coloured wool tied around your left arm. If the opposing team managed to rip off your 'life' you were then 'dead' and this disqualified you from continuing the game. If, however, you managed to reach a special tree without losing your 'life', you won. These wide games were often played at dusk to make them more exciting. They required quite a lot of guile and good hearing – I loved them.

We had some success when we put our camping skills to the test in the Delecta Camping Competition held at Phasel's Wood near Kings Langley. This was an annual weekend competition which attracted about twenty different Scout troops from the area and into which our Scout troop doggedly entered every year. The first time Steve and I took part in the competition it poured with rain all weekend, including the camp fire sing-along on the Saturday night, which was extremely soggy. You had to cook on open fires, for which you collected wood from the surrounding countryside. On a wet weekend, this caused no end of problems, as most wood we found was soaking wet. However, both Steve and I were amazed to find the team next to us always had dry wood. We observed them closely and found they had a secret store which they must have collected the week before the competition and hidden. They went on to win the competition.

The next year we trained religiously with our squad and got them used to making all the necessary gadgets out of branches of wood (like washing up racks, mug trees, etc.), which could win us points. We also had our mum make us a beef stew, which we took in preserving jars for Sunday lunch (the Scouts' motto is *Be Prepared* and we were this time). Steve was the Patrol Leader, I was the Second and the other Scouts were drawn from other patrols – Martin Hardwick, John Newman, Martin Malvisi and Ian Ashcroft.

When the big weekend came there was no van available to deliver all our camping materials to Phasels Wood, so we used the 29th's track-cart. This was a heavy wooden two-wheeled cart, which the six-boy team pulled from Oxhey to Kings Langley, a distance of about five miles. The weekend weather was varied, but our first job was to collect loads of dry wood and stow it under a tarpaulin. We pitched the tent in record time and had everything ready for inspection by the invigilators.

On Sunday it rained, but still Steve had us make an oven out of a biscuit tin, which was positioned at one end of the fireplace. He caked the tin with clay and completed it with a chimney at the back. The pre-cooked beef stew was placed in the oven and heated up. When the judges came around to inspect the meal (as they did for every team) they naturally assumed the stew had been cooked in the oven and found it delicious – we got top marks. The Delecta Shield presentation was always made with the results being announced in reverse order, and we waited anxiously for our position. We came first and won the competition (the first time in the 29th SW Herts history), and received the enormous shield. Unfortunately, there was no-one present from our troop to witness this proud event, nevertheless we hauled everything triumphantly back to Oxhey in the track cart.

Every year, around Easter, it was Bob-a-Job week. Cubs and Scouts set out to raise money by visiting their neighbours' houses and doing a job for them, for which they were paid a bob, i.e. one shilling. A shilling (twelve pence) was exactly one twentieth of a pound which doesn't sound like much nowadays, but if we consider it in today's money, accounting for inflation, it would be about £2.50. Jobs involved cutting lawns, weeding flower-beds, and running errands. When the task was completed and you had received your 'bob' you gave the person a sticker to put in their window. The sticker was a yellow colour with a red tick which showed the house had been 'done'. You had a card to list the jobs and the money received and you had to take it all completed back to the pack or troop.

The Scouts also raised money for the church by having jumble sales. We would spend evenings in the week and

Saturday mornings, touring Oxhey to collect unwanted stuff from people's houses. This could be furniture, clothes, shoes, books or anything else people didn't want anymore. We used the track-cart to make the collection and then brought it all back and stored it temporarily in the Scout hut. On the following Saturday afternoon, we had the jumble sale in the community centre and all the items were arranged on different stalls. Older Scouts were asked to staff the stalls and take the money. I normally was on the shoe stall.

The stalls were organised on Saturday morning and then at 3pm the doors to the community centre were opened. I was always amazed at the throng of people who made a mad rush to be first in. It was pandemonium for the first hour with people grabbing shoes and trying them on, not giving them back if they did not fit, and generally arguing over the purchases. The older women were the worst. There was a cake stand, a jam and chutney stand and a tea stand. After about 4.30pm things calmed down a bit and you could go and get a cup of tea and a slice of cake. Then all the things that hadn't been sold were either put on a bonfire and burnt up in an area between the Scout hut and the community centre, or taken to the scrap merchants in Watford. Panther let us select things which were not sold and take them home, if we wanted to. I remember once taking home eight paper-back books from the *The Saint* series by Leslie Charteris.

Steve left the Scout troop when he was sixteen years old. I think the lure of teenage life, girls of course, his apprenticeship in London and studying at technical college were all so far from the Oxhey Scout life that he just lost interest. Later I gained my First Class badge and, like Steve, I needed a change too. Harry Hart was disappointed with us both as he had rather counted on us becoming future Scouting assistants. I tried to explain to him I had fallen out with religion and found it difficult to go to church and to pretend to believe in God. Scouts have simple creeds which Baden Powell invented when he formed the Scout Movement in 1910. During the 1950s a promise was repeated at every Cub or Scout Meeting which was:

I promise to do my best,
To do my duty to God and the Queen.
To keep to rules of the Wolf Cub Pack/Boy Scout Troop
And to do a good turn to somebody every day.

My problem, I explained to Harry, was the God bit and attending Oxhey Church to say prayers and sing hymns. I didn't believe in it. He said not to worry – it didn't matter. But it did to me, so I left.

However, I was always grateful to Harry Hart and Dave Garrett. They selflessly gave so much of their spare time to instil in young boys the Scout's programme of informal education, with its emphasis on practical outdoor activities, including camping, woodcraft, hiking, and sports. Also, the goal of Scouting is *to contribute to the development of young people in achieving their full physical, intellectual, social and spiritual potentials as individuals, as responsible citizens and as members of their local, national and international communities.* The people who managed our Cubs and Scouts provided me with someone to look up to. I think personal inspiration is important when you are young. The Scout Movement provides this through pragmatic example by well-intentioned people.

Now the Scout Movement has gone through all sorts of changes to keep pace with those that occur as time roles by, and in the UK, Christian religious belief is no longer necessary in order to be a Scout. Cubs are now called Cub Scouts.

I hope the emphasis from Baden Powell on woodcraft, camping and hiking is still maintained. Who knows when you just might get lost and need to *Be Prepared*?

1939 Army Ordnance Survey Map of southern England,
with case and photo of my Dad.

Aerial view of Carpenders Park circa 1948. Carpenders Avenue in centre, Penrose Avenue to the left and Carpenders Park Station at the bottom of photo.

Photo courtesy of Arthur Hall

Carpenders Park Station circa 1945.

Photo courtesy of Arthur Hall

94, St. George's Drive about 1940.

100, St. George's Drive hit by a bomb in the Second World War.

Photo courtesy of Arthur Hall

Dave, Mum and Steve 1946.

Dave having a bath in the
kitchen sink 1945.

Dave, School Photo 1951.

Steve, School Photo 1949.

St. George's Drive, St. George's Day, about 1950. Front row from right: Steve Taylor-Jones, John Rowe, Derek O'Sullivan, Dave Taylor-Jones, Kenny Clarke, Kathleen Clarke, Derek Clarke, Unknown, Pamela Rowe, Linda Webb, Jean Farris and many little Bo Peeps. Back row from the right: Peter Lombardi, Paul Bitmead, Barbara Scheive, John Heathcote, Colin Heathcote, Janet Eyre, Janet Snowden.

St. George's Drive
Street Party 1947.

The Parade with Farr's News Agents, Carpenders Park 1955. *Photo courtesy of Arthur Hall*

Dave the paperboy 1957.   **Boy Scouts 1958.**

Delecta Shield Winners 1958
Back row: John Newman, Martin Malvisi, Steve, Dave
Front: Martin Hardwick, Ian Ashcroft.

Victoria Second Year School Eleven 1957-58
Back: C. Langley, K. Carpenter, Unknown, Mr. Tomblin
Middle: Unknown, R. Keeler, Unknown, J. Edgar, Unknown, Unknown, K. Fowler
Front: M. Hopkins, D. Taylor-Jones, M. Brisbane, M. Martindale, Unknown.

The Illustrious Senior Eleven 1960-61
Back: D. Taylor-Jones, C. Heathcote, P. Wright, P. Lombardi, B. Mitcham
Front: P. Hancock, J. Edgar, D. Elson, J. McLean, F. Amor.

Victoria Secondary Modern Prize Giving Ceremony 1961
(5 Upper GCE Class)
Back row, from left to right: J. McLean, D. Broom, P. Hancock,
P. Kingsley, D. Taylor-Jones, C. Heathcote, R. Knight
Front row, from left to right: R. Gilmour, N. Timms, D. Batchelor,
Lord Lingren (Guest Speaker), F. Amor.

French Trip 1960 –
Commer Camper van and lunch in a café.

Reims Cathedral.

Postcard 1960.

Dear Mum & Dad, & Pam, & Deb, (and)
after a pleasant crossing
we arrived at ~~Dover~~ Boulogne
at 6 P.M. on a smashing Boat.
The Beauvais school is huge
and very modern. The meals
are typically french and very
nice. This morning we came to
Rheims where I am writing this
to you from the inside of the cathedral. Tomorrow we are going to
go to the country. The scenery is
marvellous and very flat with white
again on Tuesday.
Love Dave. ♥xxxx

Cemetery lake and waterfall.
Photos courtesy of Arthur Hall

Steve and his BSA 250cc 1959.

Victor, Mum, Steve, Carole and Vanessa on the
BSA Shooting Star.

My Dad's old boots.

Getting Around

Over the last seventy years, since the Second World War, people's mobility has increased enormously. Back in the 50s, if people could afford holidays they stayed in their own country and only those with sufficient money could afford to venture abroad. Almost everyone travelled by public transport which was nationalized and affordable, unlike car ownership which was expensive. Nowadays, we are all used to having our own cars and the freedom to go almost anywhere we want.

My stepfather often worked nights at the Sun Printers in West Watford and his work times didn't coincide with the train's timetable. In 1953 he bought a Ford 8 car to get over this problem and it became his pride and joy. Occasionally, in the summer, he would take us for picnics to Chipperfield Common and Sarratt. When I was eight, he took us in 'Freddy the Ford' all the way to Bude, in Cornwall – it took eleven hours and two punctures. We stayed in caravans, saw the Atlantic Ocean for the first time and enjoyed wonderful weather. My parents having a car broadened my horizons a little.

I had my very first bike, which was a tricycle, as a Christmas present when I was seven. At that time the concrete road surface of St. George's Drive was in a terrible state. There were massive ruts and large parts of the road had potholes 100 to 150 mm deep. One day I went speeding down the hill and just before Compton Place, on the right-hand side, I went into a huge rut caused by the erosion of a construction joint. My front wheel went in and didn't come out, but I did, over the handlebars, landing hard on the road. I howled my way back home with blood streaming down my shirt, to be patched up and cuddled by my mum. I was one of those accident-prone children, as many second sons are, always trying to keep up with my older brother, I suppose.

When I was twelve years old it seemed there was nothing more important than owning a proper bicycle. I needed it to get around, to get away from home to visit friends, to ride to play football for the school on Saturday mornings and to ride to Bushey to attend Scout evenings. In short, it freed me from waiting for the train or bus.

Steve had made his own bike, not the frame of course, this he found in a ditch along Oxhey Lane. When he was twelve, he found a job doing a paper round and without a bike it was a lot more arduous, so he needed one quite urgently. At this time my parents didn't have the money to buy him one, so being a practical boy who loved mechanical things, he decided to salvage the frame and buy all the other parts new, piece by piece, when he could afford them.

Later, my parents managed to buy me a second-hand twenty-four inch wheel bicycle, which I rode until I was twelve, but by then I needed a bigger bike and I too had a paper round. Steve suggested we could build one together.

When he had been building his bike, we spent a lot of time in the evenings with our noses pressed to the windows of the bicycle shop in South Oxhey. New bikes were out of our league, but their shiny pedals, handlebars, lamps, derailleur gears, bells and all the other accessories were much admired and coveted. Bit by bit Steve bought what he needed for his bike and in about three months had finished assembling it. He painted it blue.

For my bike, as he had done before, Steve borrowed some tools from our Uncle John, next door at 96 St. George's Drive and, if he didn't have them, he asked Cyril Henshaw who lived across the alley from us at 92. Then once again we went hunting for a bicycle frame and found one in the ditch, this time beside Little Oxhey Lane. We couldn't understand why people threw such things away instead of taking them to George Ausden's scrap metal yard at the bottom of Watford High Street where they could get money for them.

When we got the frame home Steve took apart the pedal bearing race and examined the little ball bearings which allowed the pedals to turn smoothly. He pronounced them suitable, they just needed greasing. There were already two good pedal shafts so we went to the bicycle shop where I only needed to buy two new pedals and put them on.

Steve also took apart the bearing races under the handle-bar column, above the front forks. They received the same treatment and were greased well and re-assembled.

Then I rubbed down the frame and painted it green. Next, I bought two new twenty-six inch wheels, inner tubes and tyres – it was starting to look like a bike. As soon as I had enough money, I bought a saddle, handlebars, brakes and finally a chain. Then, at last, I could try out my bike and adjust the saddle position and brakes. I cycled around St. Meryl Estate feeling great. I was a little bit small for a twenty-six inch wheel – my feet could only just touch the ground when I was sitting on the saddle. I left the bike without mudguards for a few weeks, but after riding home from school in wet conditions I became soaked through from the wheel spray. So, the bike became equipped with white mudguards and I bought a yellow cycle cape as well, to protect me from the rain.

This bike lasted me for three years of cycling. I became adept at mending punctures, although borrowing Mum's dinner spoons to use as tyre levers wasn't always appreciated.

When I was fifteen, I bought a second-hand classic British racing bike for £15, an A.S. Gillott from the bike shop on South Oxhey estate. I had the frame professionally resprayed in a light green colour. It had narrow, lightweight wheels and no gears, just a fixed wheel and pedals with toe clips. I discovered the fixed wheel gave you much more control and with the toe clips you could pull hard going up severe hills, like Old Redding. Old Redding leads from Oxhey Lane up to Stanmore Common and is a steep hill for about a mile. It is probably one of the loveliest beauty spots in that area and from the top has an unsurpassed view over north-west London.

On my Gillott I could make the journey from home to school in Addiscombe Road, Watford, in ten minutes, even with stops at traffic lights. I started to build leg muscle and at the weekends I used to ride first to St. Albans and then on to Luton and back. Eventually I managed to ride the thirty kilometres to Luton in just over an hour.

Although nothing to do with bikes but still on the subject of getting around, when I was fifteen, we had the chance to go on a school trip to France for a week. Twelve boys squeezed into a Commer Campervan to make our first journey to 'the continent'. We were driven and supervised by Bernard Church (art master) and William Spouge (English master).

We visited Reims, Paris, Dreux, Chartres and Beauvais, all in a week. At Reims, we visited the huge cathedral, blackened by centuries of dirt. Now, I'm pleased to say, it has been cleaned to show off its magnificence. William Spouge insisted we broaden our culture by a visit to the champagne caves of *Tattinger* which are hewn out of the limestone bedrock and provide the ideal storage temperature for wine. We didn't get to taste any champagne but those rows of bottles stacked deep underground remain in my memory to this day. I expect some of the bottles I saw in 1960 are still there, although now at an incredible price.

We made a 'William Spouge' tour of the countryside near Reims, with him just following his nose, not looking at a map, getting a bit lost and eventually driving through a field to get back on the road. I cannot forget our lunches, often made by stopping in a village and buying baguettes of bread, stuffing them with camembert cheese and fresh ham bought from the butchers. It all tasted so different, the butter was unsalted and the milk much creamier.

We did not stop in Paris but drove right through the centre, over the Seine, passing the Eiffel Tower to find Dreux, a town west of Paris, where Spouge and Church wanted to show us a modern church. It had abstract, stained glass windows and Spouge pointed out how starkly it contrasted with Reims. We continued to Chartres and spent the day visiting its beautiful cathedral, climbing up one of the spires to look over the flat corn fields surrounding the town.

We stayed most of the time at a modern Catholic boarding school in Beauvais. The French schoolboys were on their summer holidays and we were allowed to sleep in their dormitories. We were lucky to be there on July 14th, Bastille Day, when a holiday atmosphere enlivened the town. This was my first visit abroad and I was strongly influenced by it.

I gave my racing bike to my younger brother Victor, as I progressed to a motor scooter and much later it was with him, unfortunately, that the A.S. Gillott met its demise. The condition of St. George's Drive was just so bad Vic had to cycle on the pavement and one day when for an instant he looked down, a car suddenly reversed out of its driveway. He hit it and sailed over the handlebars onto the car's bonnet. This impact didn't seem to damage Vic or the car but it did break the bike's crossbar clean through ending any more cycling.

Steve bought a BSA 250cc motorbike when he started work in Cricklewood. He went to work on it every day, but after a couple of years he progressed to a BSA Shooting Star 500cc twin – a super beast. We went on holiday to Devon and Cornwall on it, camping most of the time. We made a long journey crossing southern England to the Norfolk Broads, where Steve's girlfriend was on holiday.

On the return journey to London we joined the newly built M1, Britain's first motorway. We went rather fast for a short stretch, nearly one hundred miles per hour if I remember correctly. Then at a slower speed we cruised along nearing Luton when the back tyre blew out. Steve heroically managed to control the bike, as the back wheel slid around making us 'waltz' about on the road surface. We slowed to about thirty miles per hour before he was forced to leave the concrete road surface and take the bike onto the cinder hard shoulder next to the road. Here he immediately lost control on the loose surface and the bike slid from under us, spinning around on its front and back crash bars with us still on it. It stopped finally and we got off without serious injuries, except Steve had sprained his ankle. We phoned for assistance, the bike was lifted onto the back of a pick-up truck and we were ferried home to Carpenders Park. The bike was only superficially damaged, which Steve, as usual, took care of.

When I was eighteen, I had a girlfriend who lived in Haringey, near Tottenham, which meant I had to make long detours on the London Underground to see her. I needed my own transport, so I bought a scooter, a Rumi 125cc twin. Rumi is an Italian make and I bought their 'Tipo Sport' model. The Rumi was unusual, being produced entirely (except for the front forks, crash rails and leg shields) in cast aluminium resulting in a light but rigid body construction. It was designed by Donninno Rumi, who initially sculptured it in clay before building moulds for casting the body in his aluminium factory in Bergamo, Italy.

My Rumi was red, pillar box red and like all Rumis, it sounded like a high-pitched wasp. I dread to think what our neighbours thought of the noise I made returning from Haringey at midnight, whining into our driveway, disturbing their sleep. It was my mum who suggested perhaps I could switch the motor off coming down St. George's Drive hill and coast in silently.

The Rumi was fast and for its size, quite powerful. It could easily take my girlfriend and me around. But it was slightly temperamental and sometimes refused to start. This usually occurred when I tried to come home, ending up with me pushing the damned thing up and down the road trying to bump-start it.

One wet winter's night I arrived back on my Rumi in Carpenders Park and was about to turn into St. George's Drive from Little Oxhey Lane, when a drunken driver overtook the car behind me and found me in his path. I was knocked off the scooter and careered up the road. I was concussed and woke up in an ambulance being taken to the Peace Memorial Hospital in Watford. They kept me in for the night and I was allowed to come home the next day – no bones broken. My Kangol crash helmet had saved my life, but it was ground right down on one side where it had scraped along the road surface. The Rumi was in a sorry state but Steve repaired it for me, respraying the body and replacing the broken parts. But now I wanted something bigger and stronger, so I sold it shortly afterwards in part exchange for an Ariel Arrow 250cc twin.

My Ariel Arrow was light blue and had a snazzy fibre-glass fairing which deflected the slipstream nicely. It was more reliable than the Rumi and much quicker. I expect my neighbours noticed it was also quieter. I had a different girlfriend by then who lived in Battersea and once we went to Brighton on it, my longest motorbike journey.

I changed jobs and started working in Wembley Park, riding to work on the Ariel Arrow. One day a motorist suddenly pulled out in front of me from a parked position on the left-hand side. I had to brake hard and veered to the right to avoid collision. In doing this I found a lamp post blocking my path and smacked straight into it. This time I was taken by ambulance to Edgware General Hospital with mild concussion and multiple bruises. A policeman visited me in my hospital bed and patiently explained:

"When you're hit on a motorbike it's always the rider who's hurt. When you're hit in a car, it's generally the car that's damaged, the driver is normally not hurt."

This made sense to me, so while I was laying there, I gave it some thought and decided to finish with motorbikes and buy a car. I had tasted the freedom you have when you possess your own transport and it was now an essential part of my life.

South Oxhey Fun Fair

You could hear the fairground's music from the shopping parade on St. Meryl Estate. If you went down the little concrete road which led to the cattle arch and passed under the railway, then you could even hear the cries of the people being swung around on the rides. Steve and I looked at one another – it sounded exciting.

Travelling fairs came to visit South Oxhey Estate in the spring around Whitsun and again in the summer time. They used the land next to the golf course between Prestwick Road and Hayling Road. I have tried to remember the names of the fairs; a friend remembered one of them being Flanagan's Fun Fair, which does sound familiar.

We asked our mother if we could go and she agreed, a little reluctantly, but stipulated it could only be on Saturday afternoon, not in the evening – we were, after all, only ten and twelve years old at the time. She explained we would need some money and gave us sixpence each. Steve already earned money by doing a paper round, so he said he'd take two shillings extra. Mum agreed to this, but said he would be wasting his savings.

It was a fine day, the sun shone in a blue sky and when it does this, England is one of the best places in the world to be – especially if you're going to a fun fair for the first time without your parents.

We had been to a fair once before in Harrow, with my mum and her friend Jean Brown a few years earlier. I remember it distinctly as they had one of those stalls where you bought a ticket for a penny and selected a number. Then a huge red pointer swung fast around a dial of numbers. When the pointer stopped, if someone had bought that number's ticket, they won a prize, chosen from a huge selection of goods on display which tempted passers-by to try their luck.

My mum asked me, "What's your lucky number, Dave?"

Without hesitation, I said, "Four."

So, she bought a ticket with four on it and after waiting a long time the pointer turned around and stopped at – yes, four. I won and selected an aluminium saucepan for my mum. It was still being used fifty years later when she went into a care home.

On the following Saturday Steve and I gulped down our lunch and walked quickly along St. George's Drive to Carpenders Park station, through the subway and up the steps to South Oxhey. We walked down Prestwick Road in the direction of Watford and found the fair. Steve said to keep my sixpence in my pocket and only take it out when I had to pay.

I saw quite a number of kids I knew from St. Meryl Primary School, most of them there without any money, just enjoying the fun. We wandered around looking at all the rides and stalls. We discovered the fair had several main attractions which we liked. Steve was keen on the rifle range – he reserved it for later. There were many families with children rushing about, some with toffee apples in their hands. The smell of candy floss was strong, I wanted one but decided to wait until later for it. We were surprised that all the rides were brightly lit up, even though it was a bright sunny afternoon.

We loved the dodgem track, where bumper cars were powered by electricity picked up by a ceiling contact, attached to a long pole on the car's rear. The contact sparked occasionally with a blue flash as it jumped across conductors, a great effect. We watched the cars going around and the antics of the drivers trying to bump one another.

Steve said he would pay for me to have a go, although it was clear he would be driving. Music was playing loudly all over the fair, now it was Alma Cogan's *Never do a Tango with an Eskimo*. When the cars stopped, we ran over and got in one. A lanky young man came over and took one shilling from Steve, sixpence each for the ride. I watched him as he walked cleverly among the cars, effortlessly avoiding them at the same time as collecting the money – I was sure someone would hit him. Steve was busy getting the hang of the pedal controls. There was just an accelerator and brake. I was amazed at how he seemed to know how to drive a bumper car – to my knowledge he'd never done it before.

We joined the other cars circling and our car picked up speed. Steve had his foot flat on the floor and he started to swerve to miss other cars. I was enjoying it – but kept my arms well inside the safety of the car. Then suddenly, we had to brake hard, as someone had swung their car around 180 degrees and was coming full at us. Blam! We were hit and rocked back in our seats and then, before we could get going again, two friends of mine from school, Peter Lombardi and Johnny Bishop, smacked into us from behind. Steve manoeuvred the car out and we got going again. I could see Steve's face and knew he meant to get his own back. We picked up speed and he asked me to keep an eye out for cars behind us. We swerved around, dodging everyone. It was great fun. Finally, after several circuits we saw Lombardi and Bishop's car stationary, stuck after being pranged and now trying to pull out from the side. Steve angled our car to smack them back against the side as we sped past, but before he could do it a loud hooter sounded and our car and all the rest slowed down and stopped. This was all you got for sixpence, about three minutes worth of bumping.

We watched the people coming down the Helter Skelter, a tall wooden tower structure with a staircase inside it and a chute with a waxed floor which wound its spiral way down the outside. People climbed to the top and sitting on hessian mats zoomed down the chute. You needed to be out of the way quickly at the bottom to avoid the next person colliding into you. By now Bill Haley and his Comets were belting out *Shake Rattle and Roll*. Rock 'n' Roll had arrived in South Oxhey.

We moved along with crowds of people to see the Waltzer, a big roundabout with a floor which went up and down. When the four-seater cars went around on it they were forced to go up and down at the same time. People and children were held in by a safety bar and when the roundabout gained speed, they all started to cry out long "Ohhhs" and "Ahhhs" when they were flung up and down. I wasn't too keen on this one.

My favourite ride was a chair swing roundabout, where you sat in individual chairs suspended on chains, so as the ride turned the chairs all swung outwards. It looked like it would be fun, especially when they played Eddie Calvert's *It's Cherry Pink and Apple Blossom White*, with the people soaring around to the music.

Steve met his friend Malcolm Cook and we wandered off to the rifle range. They both bought goes and were given air rifles to shoot down metal ducks, which moved past in lines. When you hit one correctly it folded backwards on its base hinge. They didn't win any prizes.

There was a small show which fascinated me. It was a circular booth with a flat table surface covering most of the inside area. A man was standing in the middle. The surface was covered in a grid of lines and you placed pennies in a wooden slotted ramp and then let them roll to see if you could get them to land inside a square, which contained a number. If you did this you won the amount in pennies. If the penny landed on a grid line, you lost. If it went too far and fell into a gutter in the middle, you lost. The man had a long tee-shaped stick which he used to rake in the 'lost' pennies. I watched as people took their chance. Most aimed for the higher scores like ten or twelve which were located farthest away. They misjudged how quickly the penny would travel and usually lost. They tended to place their pennies too high on the ramp. Having been lucky once before at the Harrow Fair I thought Lady Luck must be on my side and I could perhaps win again.

I decided to try for the ones and twos which were near to the outside edge. I changed my sixpenny piece for six individual pennies. I placed a penny near to the bottom of the ramp and aimed it at a group of ones. The penny rolled off the end and fell over almost immediately smack on the middle of a grid. Lost, it was raked away. I moved the next penny very slightly higher on the ramp and this time it landed just inside a two square, but the man said it was touching one of the outside lines and raked it away. I tried again, but my penny must have been slightly worn for it rolled on further and I lost. I decided to have a go at a six which was located midway on the table and got it first time. Six pennies were sent back to me, with a grin from the man and some muffled comment.

Just as I was about to play, a new song came on over the loud speakers – Joan Regan's *Prize of Gold* – was this a favourable omen? I tried for a three and lost narrowly. I finely adjusted the position of the penny's release on the ramp and made sure the next three pennies were all the same quality. Bingo! I scored, once, twice and then three times. I counted my pennies and found I had twelve – a shilling. It was enough for me – I quit while ahead.

I had arranged with Steve to meet him at 5pm at the biggest draw in the fun fair, a boxing tent. I watched the crowds massing before the stage in front of it. A showman paraded two boxers and invited men to come and last three rounds with one of them. He told us all about their past fights, how many knock-outs they'd had. One of the boxers fascinated me, he was big and black, a heavy-weight, I guessed. His name was Jim Louis (not to be confused with the famous Joe Louis, the Brown Bomber, but I guess this was the idea). Jim wore a big prize-belt, which was shiny silver. He looked dangerous, he didn't smile but kept making boxing gestures at the crowd and skipping up and down on his toes. His skin gleamed in the sun and he had big muscles. Who was going to be brave enough to take on this guy? They would get murdered, I thought.

The prize for lasting three rounds was £5 – this can be compared with the average salary in 1955 of £8 a week. The showman raised his voice and egged on the crowd, surely there was a hero here in South Oxhey? Suddenly, a young man stepped up and offered to challenge Jim Louis. The crowd roared its support. He was dark haired, about 1.8 metres tall and stockily built. He seemed to be known by a few people who cheered wildly for him. The showman told everyone to come back at 4.45pm to buy entry tickets. He would kit out the contender with shorts, shoes and boxing gloves. The entrance price was one shilling – I decided I would go.

I found Steve and Malcolm and told them about it. They only had six pence left each, so Steve said they would wait outside for me. We left the fair and went over to one of the dells which were nearby. There were two dells, deep depressions which were apparently formed when gravel was quarried from them during the construction of the railway line in the late 1800s. Now, one was covered in grass right down to its bottom and was about ten metres deep. The other dell was close to Hayling Road and was also deep but lined with trees and bushes. This one was of more interest to us as it had some tree roots completely exposed allowing us to squeeze in behind them and hide or pretend that we were in prison.

Near to the first dell, there was a Dare Devil High Diver show. A long ladder extended for about eight metres vertically and directly below it was a round plastic pool of water about three metres diameter and half a metre deep. You could pay to see a man dive from the top of the ladder into this shallow pool. It looked impossible, but on Sunday the High Diver would do it three times. It was difficult to believe he could dive into only fifty centimetres of water.

I showed up at the boxing tent and bought my ticket by standing behind a man, hoping they would think he was my dad. They couldn't have cared less – into the tent I went with about one hundred others. It was standing room only so, being small, I managed to get near to the front. Steve said he and Malcolm would try to see through small gaps in the tent that they'd found. I don't think I'd ever spent a shilling before. Let's not forget in 1955 one penny bought two ha'penny chews or four Black Jack sweets in Farr's News Agency and I had spent twelve times as much.

The tent filled up and its doors were closed. The two boxers were brought into the ring in the centre. The showman now became the referee and introduced the two opponents by making them shake gloves. Jim Louis looked especially good now in royal blue silk shorts and a white vest. The contender, who someone behind me said was a cockney, had on white shorts and a white singlet. Apparently, he'd just come out of the Army. Steve said normally the fights didn't last long, so he expected my shilling would only get me one round. But he was wrong.

The bell sounded and the two boxers squared up to one another. The cockney was light on his feet and moved quickly. In my opinion he would need to be very quick in order to avoid the long reach of Jim Louis' massive arms. They moved around the ring, Jim Louis stealthily lunging forward trying to get in range of his opponent. Jim tried to block the cockney in a corner, but he feinted to go one way and then went the other, slipping out and smacking Jim hard on the side of his face as he did so. Jim looked strongly at his opponent. It now appeared something more than an exhibition match was taking place. Jim renewed his attack and tried to get his arms around the cockney in a clinch, but he received a battery of fast blows to his side. I saw him screw up his face briefly. Maybe the match result was not the foregone conclusion I had expected.

The cockney backed away avoiding all the punches Jim swung at him. He was fast and it became evident he was an extremely good boxer, even though he was a weight below Jim. The first round finished without Jim Louis landing a single punch on the cockney. The showman went to talk to Jim in the break and seemed to be giving him strict orders. The cockney was sweating nicely but didn't seem to be at all ruffled. The next round went the same way, Jim trying some rather crude tactics but the cockney was just too fast and fit to be caught by any of it. And he didn't land a single punch on Jim, just weaved and bobbed for the whole round. The crowd started to shout and boo. They wanted blood. When the bell for the third round sounded, the cockney completely changed his tactics and came straight at Jim Louis. He got inside his guard quickly and gave him a number of terrible body-blows just above the stomach. I could see Jim wincing in pain and he pushed away to try and swing a punch, but before he could do so, the cockney ducked and threw an uppercut straight on the chin with his left. Jim sagged a little and before the cockney could move in to finish him off, the referee stopped the fight. The crowd went wild.

The referee obligingly held the cockney's arm aloft to show he had won. We stamped and whistled our applause for the victor. The tent doors opened and we all trooped out. I heard someone say the cockney was an Army middleweight champion.

I told Steve the story of the fight as we walked home, where we were just in time for one of my mum's famous Saturday teas – cheese and tomato sandwiches, chocolate cup-cakes and a Bakewell tart. A fitting end to a wonderful day, unless you were Jim Louis.

Bluebell Woods

When I started to work as a paperboy at Farr's News Agency, I noticed they sold maps of our area. I had been interested in maps ever since joining the Scouts, so I bought one and discovered the little stream which flows secretly under the parade of shops on St. Meryl Estate was called the Ickle. I have now learnt it is called the Hartsbourne Stream, so maybe the Ickle was a local name – I actually prefer it, so I shall use it in this essay. This stream begins somewhere above the Five Fields on the higher land at Bushey Heath, captures rainwater run-off from the fields of Brazier's Farm and then ducks under Oxhey Lane.

Back then, in the 1950s, it flowed through a wood next to Highfields, before this area of land was changed to become one of the biggest cemeteries in North London. On this side of the lane the Ickle ponded into a shallow lake before cascading on over a small waterfall. The Ickle (and it is quite small) then slips down through bluebell-carpeted woods to the bottom of Harrow Way to pass under the parade of shops at Carpenders Park.

In the 1930s when Mr. Absalom had planned St. Meryl Estate it must have been decided to cover the Ickle so the parade of shops and roads could be built over it, for just before the shops the Ickle disappears into a dark rectangular culvert for about fifty metres and then emerges on the other side of the road which leads to the station.

After this, the stream meanders down to the railway and passes under the embankment and flows onto the South Oxhey side to eventually join the River Colne near Rickmansworth, which in turn joins the Thames south of Uxbridge. If a boy was to pee into the stream, as boys do, his water would follow this course and end up in the sea at the mouth of the Thames.

The Ickle had always intrigued my brother Steve and me. With the Rowe boys from two doors up the road, we explored it in 1952. We followed a little path which I expect people from Harrow Way had made to walk their dogs, and we ventured into the woods. We found a woodpecker's hole neatly drilled into a tree and saw a kingfisher flash by. Half a mile further on we came to the waterfall, into whose top crevice a crude tin boat was lodged. Perhaps a long time ago someone had tried to float it on the lake. We felt a strange foreboding atmosphere about the place, at least that's how it seemed to our impressionable young minds. Someone said they saw a movement in the wood's depths so we all took fright and ran back down the path towards the safety of the shops. Looking back now it was as though we had taken a glimpse into the past and seen something haunting this ancient woodland area. Of course, it fascinated us.

A year or so later, in the summer, Steve and I saw a film at Saturday morning pictures about an adventure in Africa where explorers were forced to wade up a river in the jungle – it looked exciting. Our only 'river' was the Ickle, so we crossed the allotments at the bottom of

Harrow Way, took off our shoes and socks and waded in. We walked up the stream bed which was only about three inches deep and covered in smooth pebbles. It was narrow enough for a man to have jumped between the banks, but the stream was cut into the clay to a depth of two to three feet, so boys would be more or less hidden. In the summer you could see tiddlers swim in the clear water and frog spawn was collected by the children of St. Meryl School for their nature lessons. It wasn't Africa, it was Carpenders Park, but I've always had a strong imagination.

The people who owned the houses backing on to the stream from Harrow Way had built fences to terminate their land and someone had made a little opening in their fence bottom through which ducks could leave their garden and enter the water. We waded past this and squinted in to try and see the ducks but there weren't any. I asked Steve why the ducks didn't just swim away up the stream and escape. I found the answer to my question when I caught my shin on some barbed wire fixed under the water. It was a nasty gash and it bled a lot, so it was back home for us. We wouldn't be discovering much else that day.

What remains strongly lodged in my memory is the wonderful sight of the wood in the springtime when its floor was covered in bluebells. They would stretch in a light blue carpet as far as you could see, contrasting with the dark tree trunks. Their smell was a light delicious scent. Bluebells send down deep roots into the leaf mould and appear as a green swathe covering the ground in March. They need light in order to flower so they grow best under deciduous trees like beech and oak, and show their magic carpet of blue blooms at the end of April or the beginning of May, just before the trees get their leaves. People from St. Meryl Estate would gather them and come back with their arms full, something you are forbidden to do now. They must have been growing in this wood for centuries to have spread like they had.

When we grew older the wood and the land bordering both Oxhey Lane and Little Oxhey Lane was zoned for a change of use to become a cemetery. A stout wooden fence was erected around the entire plot and secure entrance gates installed in Oxhey Lane. The lake was cleaned and enlarged, the waterfall improved and a nice little bridge constructed below it. You could walk down a neat gravel path to another new entrance, made for people who came by train to Carpenders Park station. A peaceful area for mourners was created in what before had been a part of the countryside. It took some time to construct all this, and it was several years before the cemetery was in full operation – you hardly ever saw anyone being buried there or people mourning their lost loved ones. The residents of St. Meryl Estate still used to walk up the path and visit their bluebells in the spring time, just like in previous years.

Steve and I didn't like this change so we continued to enter the property by climbing over the fence. Here we would see different birds from those we spotted in the spinney behind our house including doves, magpies, jays, wood pigeons, a heron, spotted woodpeckers, and kingfishers. We also noticed a man had now been employed to be a caretaker and groundsman. We always saw him before he saw us, for we knew he would object to our being there, so we kept well clear of him when cutting through to go to the fields on the other side of Oxhey Lane. But the 'Cem', as we called it, was now forbidden territory, which of course made it even more attractive.

At the end of the Second World War St. Meryl Estate had not been completely finished. At the top of Harrow Way, the road ended in a little copse, on whose edge a farmer used to build a big haystack every summer. Compton Place should have joined Harrow Way at its top part but it too ended in the little copse. If you look on old maps there is a wooded area called Gibbs Couch Plantation exactly where this copse stopped the roads from continuing, so maybe some ancient law prohibited construction there at this time. It was only ten years after the end of the war when both roads were completed and Harrow Way joined into Little Oxhey Lane and Compton Place was connected to Harrow Way. New houses were built on these roads and the maintenance of the estate's private roads, which were in lamentable condition, was taken over by Watford Rural District Council and they were repaired and resurfaced. The same extensions and improvements were made to other parts of the estate where new bungalows were built and sold.

Steve developed an interest in hunting, well, shooting a 4.10 rifle at pigeons and squirrels, with his classmate Dan, whose dad was a farmer in Merryhill Road, Bushey. They used to spend their Sundays touring the fields, Dan with his 12 bore, Steve with Dan's 4.10, mostly in the pouring rain. I suppose it was inevitable Steve would want a gun of his own, but there was no doubt neither my mum nor our stepfather would allow it. However, Steve bought an air rifle from someone in his class at school and hid it in our attic, so they wouldn't find it.

In fact, although there were only eighteen months between Steve and me, when he was fourteen I think he thought I was still a kid, so he didn't tell me either. Our bedroom was in the roof of our bungalow and there was a small door in the side wall which gave access to the water tank. It was in here I found Steve's secret, pushed under the bedroom floor between the ceiling joists. I waited to let him know about how I had discovered another of his secrets, too.

One day I was staring out of the dormer window of our bedroom onto a rainy garden when I turned back to the room and noticed something odd, secreted in the back of an old radio we had picked up at a Scouts' jumble sale. These radios were operated by valves which used to get hot, so the back panel of the radio was made of cardboard with slotted ventilation holes. Pressed against this back, clearly visible against the grille, were some books. I opened up the radio to discover *The Woman of Rome* by Albert Moravia, and a couple of other rather 'hot' looking books. I held up one by its spine and the pages swung open at a favourite spot so I could read the sexy bits which Steve enjoyed when I was not there, "His hand caressed her silken knee…" etc.

I told him about my finds to let him know I was not as young as he thought and knew about his secrets. So, in the Easter holidays he let me accompany him when his school friend came over to visit, bringing his air pistol, too. Steve decided we would all go shooting on the Five Fields, as he and Dan did at the weekends. We nipped through the cemetery, easily avoiding the groundsman, crossed Oxhey Lane and entered the fields. I was dying to have my turn with the rifle but did not want to shoot any birds, so I just shot at a fence post.

Air rifles work by compressing a spring when you break the barrel to reload. This in turn compresses air which is released behind a little lead 0.22 pellet when you pull the trigger and shoot the gun. It's not dangerous unless you use specially shaped pellets – we only had simple rounded ones. These were not enough to kill a large bird, only a very small one like a sparrow.

Anyway, we messed around a bit and then came back through the Cem by climbing over the fence on Oxhey Lane. I was behind Steve and his friend, who were probably talking about girls or motorbikes, when all of a sudden from out of a bush jumped the groundsman and grabbed Steve by the arm.

"S'pose you thought you were being clever coming in here, did'ya? S'pose you thought I hadn't seen you? Well I've got you now and I see you've guns and have been hunting on this land. That's against the law. I'm calling the police to charge you," he blurted out.

Sliding carefully behind some rhododendron bushes, I hid myself and watched through the leaves. Steve and his mate were marched off to the office near the lake and the police were called. I guessed Steve would realise there was nothing I could do, so taking a circuitous route I scarpered back home and waited. About an hour later a policeman called at our house with the boys and their air guns. Mum was livid with Steve. He received a right dressing down, from both her and our stepfather. The gun was confiscated and sold. I was sworn to secrecy by Mum not to mention the incident to anyone at school or at Scouts.

A summons was received for Steve and his friend to appear at Watford Magistrate's Court for illegally using firearms on the cemetery property. Steve felt bad about letting his friend down, and for letting Mum down too. For a few weeks a feeling of gloom settled over us both, as I was included in all this by association.

But after some time, the atmosphere lightened when the parents of Steve's friend telephoned to say they had taken a solicitor to represent the boys at court. Both parents agreed to split the legal costs.

In the end Steve and his friend went to a hearing at court but never had to appear before the Magistrate, the case being thrown out on a technicality found by the solicitor. Air rifles are not firearms apparently, so the case was dismissed. Quite right too, they hadn't actually done anything wrong, hadn't fired their guns in the cemetery and the over-zealous groundsman should have just given them a ticking off for climbing over the fence and explained that cemeteries are not a place for children to be without their parents.

Time passed, the kids grew up and the parents grew old. What has not changed and continue to appear in all their beauty every year, no matter what, are the wonderful bluebells growing next to the Ickle/Hartsbourne stream flowing through these ancient woods.

Uncle John

I suppose if you were asked, "Who was the most influential person in your life?", you would need to pause and think a bit. For me, several people helped and influenced me at different times. However, if I remember my childhood, outside of my immediate family, there is one person who stands out – my Uncle John.

When my mum and dad bought their semi-detached bungalow in Carpenders Park in 1937, my mum's brother John and his wife Jean decided to buy the house next door – the mirror image bungalow. This strikes me now as a bit strange and perhaps even invasive in terms of privacy, but when you consider they were both born in New Cross, in south east London, where most of the houses were terraced, then having only one house attached to yours must have been quite a change. Perhaps being brother and sister, only a couple of years apart in age, made them rather close. So, we lived at 94 and they lived at 96.

Across the driveway, which separated 94 from 92, lived Cyril Henshaw and his wife who he called Bill, with daughters Pat and Chrissie. John, my dad and Cyril all became good friends and helped one another out when getting their gardens straight and doing all those things necessary when you buy a new house. Chrissie, who is now in her eighties, told me she found John rather handsome and she had quite a crush on him when she was thirteen. I can understand why, he was tall and good-looking.

John was a master joiner and he had built himself a large garage in his garden, which extended into a woodwork shop where he took refuge from his difficult and explosive wife, Jean. They had a daughter, Janet, who was their only child.

When my dad was killed at the end of the Second World War, my mum was fortunate to have her younger brother living right next door, as I am sure she needed his support. My brother Steve and I grew up with Uncle John as a sort of occasional surrogate father, although Auntie Jean never allowed him to get too close to us. Perhaps he longed for a son and she was wary of him developing too close a bond with us.

Uncle John was a strong character, a bit like my mum and he was kind enough to do all sorts of little jobs for us when he could. I remember spending rainy days with him in his garage and hearing the rain pound on the corrugated asbestos sheeting roof, as he showed me his carpentry tools. The workshop smelt of cut wood and glue. John was a meticulous man and always cleaned up his wood shavings after work and collected them in a box for the fire. It felt safe and secure in there. He used to smoke quite a lot, like most men of his time and he preferred roll-up cigarettes. He would take a break from whatever he was doing, get out a tin of tobacco and expertly, without looking at it, roll a cigarette, wetting the paper with his lips. He seemed to enjoy his fags a lot.

One day when we were in the garage, he gave me a pin hammer, a small tenon saw and some bits of wood and asked me what I wanted to make. "Lamp-posts," I said. He showed me how to cut little bits of wood for a base, longer bits for the post and little bits for the lights. Then he showed me how to nail the pieces together. They didn't actually resemble lamp-posts, but they kept me busy for a couple of hours. John had a thin moustache and dark straight hair, which he wore swept back. He had a droll sense of humour and often had Steve and me roaring with laughter.

He owned a shooting-brake car and had hand-made its wooden exterior bracing which was all the rage in the 1950s. The car looked smashing, with its polished wooden struts reinforcing the grey bodywork. He also made the housing for his TV set in curved plywood. I suppose he steamed the sheets of plywood to bend them, forming gentle rounded corners which contained the television tube and screen. The result looked so professional. He made a TV table with tubular chrome legs and a veneered French polished top which, after some years when Jean tired of it, was passed on to us. I loved and prized it.

My mum was a competent cook and we were brought up on shepherd pies, Cornish pasties, meat pies with golden crusty pastry and all sorts of cakes and puddings. Occasionally, when John popped through the garden gate, built into the timber fence separating our two gardens, Mum would give him a taste of something she had just baked. But he couldn't let Jean know – it had to remain a secret. Jean had red hair and a terrible temper to go with it. She became jealous over the simplest things my mum did for John. We boys were made part of their conspiracy and instructed never to say Uncle John had just eaten some of the cupcakes or other treats which had come freshly out of Mum's oven.

You would have thought when my mum married again, Jean's jealousy would have been laid to rest, but she never seemed to get over it. Mum and her new husband Stan had twins, Victor and Vanessa, and it was not long before our little two-bedroomed bungalow became too small to contain everyone. In 1955 my parents had a room made in the loft and a dormer window created in the roof. This provided a bedroom for Steve and me. Sometimes Uncle John would come around to see us in the evening and I remember him climbing up the ladder to our new bedroom.

We had devised a game, with marbles and books, where the books were made into a long shallow slope and you had to roll marbles down to hit others below. He loved this and, like a big kid, joined us in the game. But he kept up a running commentary of jokes and laughs, telling us, "This is serious play, you know," which made us laugh even more. Auntie Jean decided she must have a third bedroom too and so Uncle John, having just finished redecorating the complete house in pastel shades, made a superb staircase and dormer bedroom in his roof as well.

John's garden was, like ours, flat at the bottom with a lawn and then a steep rockery slope, up to a second flat area, which ended in a fence. Behind this fence was a spinney and an embankment cutting for the London and Midland Region Line railway. John decided to create a lawn on his top area which meant building a wall between his land and ours, about a metre high and twenty metres long. He did this by building timber shuttering and filling it with concrete. He had no concrete mixer, but mixed the concrete by hand outside his garage and then carried it in two buckets, one in each hand. He had to lift this heavy load up the rockery steps, cross to the construction and then tip it into the wall shutters. It was back-breaking work and it took him about six full weekends to do it. I admired his strength and fortitude. I guess he was about thirty-eight years old at the time and very hard-working.

One time, when he was gardening on his side of the fence, I was watching him and enjoying a bag of lemon sherbet, sticking in my finger and licking it off. It had just been raining and he produced a large earthworm from the clay and showed it to me.

"I'll give you ten shillings," he said, "if you dare to dip the worm into the sherbet and then suck it."

Ten shillings was an enormous amount of money to me, so I reached for the worm. I was about to dip it into the sherbet when he said, "Hold it good and tight, Dave. You don't want to lose it and have it slide down your throat."

I gag now at the thought. I just couldn't do it and this amused him greatly.

In the 1950s, on November 5th, Bonfire Night, you could build a bonfire at home and let off your own fireworks. Our family always celebrated this event, with Steve and I making a big fire on the top terrace of our garden. As our stepfather used to work nights he was never there for this evening, so Uncle John would join in and supervise the fire. We used to have friends and neighbours over to join us and this increased the number of fireworks which were let off. Olive used to make sausage rolls, cheese straws, toffee apples and soup which we drank from mugs. Uncle

John would make sure we did not burn ourselves when the Catherine-wheels failed to turn, or if roman candles fell over and shot flaming balls across the lawn. I think he enjoyed it as much as we did.

When Steve and I were young teenagers, Uncle John invented a game he called 'Battyball'. We played it on his lower lawn and it was a form of tennis. He strung a net midway across the lawn and made bats out of plywood. These were about 400 mm long and looked like big wide spoons. We played in singles or doubles (if another boy could be found) and you just had to hit a small rubber ball over the net for the opponent to hit back. It sounds a bit simple, but Uncle John made it such fun and with all his funny comments we would fall about laughing. When we stopped for a break, we would have a cup of tea, on a long seat under his glass veranda. One time when Auntie Jean was absent, my mum made individual black-currant puddings, served in china bowls, liberally laced with caster sugar to accompany the tea. I can still see Uncle John's face now as he relished the treat.

Steve went into production engineering, starting an apprenticeship in a factory in London and when it became my turn to leave school, I was faced with the difficult choice of what career to follow. Initially I had the idea of being a land surveyor but with Uncle John's help and suggestions, I wrote to several civil engineering contractors and finally secured a position.

My life changed and I spent my time working in London, attending day release and night school and seeing my steady girlfriend. It was my mum who informed us seriously one evening that Uncle John had lung cancer and was being hospitalised. I was so shocked when she took us to see him a few weeks later at the Peace Memorial Hospital in Watford. He lay in bed, very thin, his skin a yellow colour against the white sheets. It seems he had left it much too late, soldiering on at work while the disease progressed. The cancer had metastasized throughout his body quickly and the strong, clever master joiner, who was my uncle, succumbed to it within a fortnight. He was only forty-five years old.

After his death, relations with Auntie Jean and Janet soured quickly. Five years later they moved away and we never heard from them again.

Saturday Afternoon Window Shopping
in Watford

When I was seventeen years old, I used to spend Saturday afternoons either going with my friend Peter Hancock to watch Watford FC play football, or, if they had an away fixture, going window shopping in Watford High Street. Both of us were rather fashion conscious and in 1962, as we were both at work, we could afford to save up for a new suit, an overcoat or new shoes. There was great pleasure to be had in looking in the windows of the men's outfitters and imagining what we would look like in the clothes which we fancied. But as we didn't earn much, we only bought occasionally, after long weeks of looking and making decisions.

At this time shopping malls didn't exist and the only places to buy new clothes were the High Street shops. Watford was a town of about seventy-five thousand people and had a long High Street. The Lower High Street was not of much interest to us, as it was an area of electrical repair shops, garages and petrol stations – no clothes shops. After Watford High Street station, going up the hill past Cramer's wonderful toy shop, against whose window I had pressed my nose ever since I was a little kid to gaze in awe at the model planes and trains, the shops started to get much more interesting. Just before Water Lane, on the left-hand side was a Jewish tailor who always had new stock and featured a lot of rather Italian influenced designs. Some of the jackets were so short, they were called 'bum freezers' and were considered rather daring. Peter and I would stand in the plate glass entrance foyer, looking at the jackets and the owner always tried hard to attract us inside, but we never bought anything there – it was too flash for us.

We would then saunter on up the High Street, past Rossi's Ice Cream Bar to Burton's on the corner of King Street. Here things began to get more serious. Burton's had made-to-measure suits and overcoats of quality. However, my first suit was bought in 1961 from John Collier's and was a dark graphite grey, single-breasted affair. I know it was a bit sombre, but I needed it for our dancing lessons at Oakley Studios where Peter was joined by his girlfriend Julie, and I tagged along as we tried to learn how to dance. I think we stuck it out for a year. We progressed through the waltz, the quick-step (a bit more difficult) and then to the dreaded foxtrot. Pete and Julie made good progress as they were always dancing together and, hey, let's face it, they had a good sense of timing. For me of course, the whole reason to learn ballroom dancing was to meet girls. Being single, I always had a different partner, but rarely were they someone I liked dancing with. I'm an average-sized guy, but I always seemed to get tall or small partners. The only dance I really liked was the cha-cha-cha. In my dark suit I felt much more confident and could one-two cha-cha-cha, back-two cha-cha-cha away with the best of them.

Peter's first suit was a double-breasted grey and blue mix, slightly Italian – very 'raz'. He had rather luxuriant, dark, wavy hair, and like all of us at this time, he combed it straight back without a parting. With his charm and wonderful smile, he did come over as a little bit Italian. But, mind you, only when he wore the suit.

Christmas time in Watford was special, as the town put up electric light decorations which, during the 1950s and early 60s, always seemed to be the same ones. However, when these garlands were suspended across the street, they changed the town so much we always looked forward to them. At Queen's Road, the High Street got busy with a Woolworths, Boots the Chemist and a wonderful old fresh coffee shop, whose delicious aroma of roasting coffee beans pervaded the street.

Then you came to where Peter lived in St. Mary's Road, just behind the old St. Mary's flint-stone church, which does not quite make it onto the High Street, but was in a charming old square of alms houses and ancient pavements, which you accessed on your left just after Lyon's Corner House. The old High Street was necked at this point and traffic squeezed through to arrive at an enlarged area which was the site of the old Watford Cattle Market. After the Second World War, there was too much traffic to allow the market to stay there, so it was moved behind a large department store called Cawdells. This widened area had a couple of banks and finer buildings around it, some with exposed stonework. Market Street was an important road which joined the old market square with a nice pub, the Compasses, next door to Watford Post Office. A little further up the High Street on the right was the Gaumont

Cinema, where Peter, Julie and I would go to see touring rock 'n' roll groups. Normally, of course, we went to the cinema on Saturday nights if there wasn't anything else to do.

The aspect of the High Street changed after Market Street junction. The shops became larger and a little more prestigious. A few important banks, lawyers' offices and estate agents' premises occupied cream stucco Georgian buildings. Just after Clarendon Road, with its Watford Palace Theatre, on the left just before the fire station, was our favourite record shop where we would spend long hours browsing through the LPs. The High Street then continued past the fire station and Clements, the largest department store in the town and then past the town car park to a more gracious road arrangement, where the shops were set back on the right-hand side to allow an ornamental pond in front of the Odeon Cinema. Some of the shops were rather picturesque, situated in buildings probably constructed before the twentieth century. The High Street terminated in a roundabout in front of the Watford Town Hall.

Peter and I rarely went to this upper High Street area to window shop as there were few clothes shops, unless it was to go to the Odeon Cinema or to Spivey's sport shop.

Peter's house at 84, St. Mary's Road was Victorian and terraced, with attractive coloured brickwork. For me it was a sort of haven in the town. Although it was a small house it had a special atmosphere, friendly and open. Mrs. Hancock always had time for a word with me and to offer a cup of tea. Their lounge had a coal fire giving off a friendly blaze and there was the wonderful radiogram on which we played all our favourite records.

When I was at Victoria Secondary Modern Boys School with Peter, it was just too risky to leave my bike in the cycle sheds – it would be stripped in a day. Peter's mum allowed me to keep it in their tiny back garden during the day after I had cycled from my home to school. I would arrive at about 8.40am and walk to school with Peter. I think it was these walks every day to school and back and the little stop-over at his house which laid the foundations for our life-long friendship.

After we left school and started work, Peter in Watford and me in London, I used to pop in when I was in the town at the weekends. Sometimes I would stay over with Peter on Saturday night and we would spend hilarious evenings eating grapefruits in bed and keeping his parents awake with our barely-contained laughter.

But back to the window shopping. My first overcoat was light grey, made of fine wool which almost bordered on pale blue. It was knee-length. Peter's was a grey fleck and quite short, in the modern style. Overcoats only got shorter in the 1960s, it wasn't until the early 1970s that they got longer again and started to scrape the ground. Ties were a big fashion statement and at this time were quite thin with horizontal stripes of patterned colour. You had to have quite a few of them to alternate with your suit. At one time, woollen crocheted ties became the rage, made of loose stitches of thick wool. To save money, my mum handmade me several. Just after I started work, I sat down in an Italian restaurant in Queensway and my crochet tie fell in my minestrone soup. It almost drained the bowl.

It was a wonderful feeling going back to Peter's house and trying on our new clothes in front of Mrs. Hancock and Jennifer, Peter's younger sister. It was as if I had become an accomplished young man, rather than a boy. Julie had a Saturday job in a shop, so at the end of the day she would often be there to approve our latest possessions. Years later, when I moved to Nice in the South of France, Peter and Julie used to come on holiday and sometimes Peter and I would go to a large shopping mall called *Cap 3000* and tour the shops, trying on clothes, just like we had all those years before.

Peter's dad seemed to be always working when I visited, but I remember him being there a couple of times. He invited me into their tiny front room and put some Hawaiian music on his wind-up gramophone. He would play along to the music with some bones, polished cream flat ones, which he held in a special way in his hands. He clicked them fast in time to the music. He had a special talent. He introduced me to Django Reinhardt, the great jazz guitarist – I will never forget him playing *Nuages* on the gramophone and expertly clicking along to the music.

How Watford developed in the 1970s and later was a disappointment to many people. Charming aspects were sacrificed in the interests of town planning and traffic circulation. It became ugly, although the top part of the town has recently been made pedestrian to good effect. Well done, Watford, for this change, but I would like to see all the old High Street from Water Lane onwards, made pedestrian.

Personal memories are important when you get older. They evoke the passing of time, but let's not forget it's *your* time, a period that was a part of *your* life. Watford was a good town to be young in during the early 1960s, as what had formed it architecturally was still evident. It is a large Hertfordshire market town, with a long past. However, appreciating architecture which is from our own time is not always evident. Conversely, we can quite easily be attracted to things from previous eras to ours. Like choosing antiques, old things are often safe choices while things from our own time aren't always as easy to like. Modern architecture doesn't often hold the same appeal to us as old buildings, yet our children will probably appreciate it as (I am convinced) it is not from their time.

I think I prefer my childhood memories of Watford. And nostalgic preference probably holds good for our parents and forebears – they might have preferred the environment of their past times too. I think that's why, when we're older, memories cocoon us into believing our early times were better than the present one we are living in.

Musical Influences

I started to listen to music with my mother and brother, cuddled up on her lap listening to a radio programme for young children called '*Listen with Mother*', probably in 1950. This was on at a quarter to two every afternoon, when children had finished their lunch and were getting ready for an afternoon nap. There were nursery rhymes and a little story and I can remember being upset when it finished – I loved it and wanted more. My brother Steve and I would sing along with our mother and soon learnt these little tunes, which have been sung by children for centuries in England.

My mother had a record player, which had been put together by my father. It had a turntable with an electric motor and was assembled in a wooden cabinet. It played through loud speakers that were fitted in the radio and positioned above it. The pick-up had metallic needles, which were not like the resistant diamond ones of later models, so they wore out after a few plays and then had to be changed. You put a record on the turntable and then manually lowered the pick-up onto the record as it turned around. Most records we had were 78s. We had one record which was smaller, about 100 mm diameter, and this was Jack Payne's '*Say it with Music*'. It wasn't interesting for us as it was a promotion record for his band. One of our best loved songs was '*The Teddy Bear's Picnic*' by Henry Hall. I fell in love with this record at an early age.

My mother had albums of records in 78s format, some of which she started to collect when she worked for an HMV record store in the Harrow Road, near Edgware Road tube station in London, before the war. These albums had stiff-backed cardboard covers with paper sleeves to hold the discs. The 78s albums were quite big and heavy and looked like thick encyclopedias. Some were classical music and others popular music. She had two big albums by Bing Crosby, who must have been my parent's favourite singer.

Steve and I were allowed to use the record player under my mother's supervision. I remember listening to her music mostly on rainy days when we couldn't go outside to play. I think the song which had sold the most records worldwide by the 1950s was Bing Crosby's '*I'm Dreaming of a White Christmas*', which was in one of Mum's albums, but my strongest memories of her music were two other Crosby numbers, '*Dear Hearts and Gentle People*' and '*Mule Train*', which were back to back on the same record. This record was released in October 1949, with *Dear Hearts* as the A side and *Mule Train* as the B side. I think this record could have been bought for Mum by her second husband Stan.

Mule Train was one of the first records to have sound effects on it, such as whip cracks, and it was a big favourite with Steve and me. We would sit astride the arms of the sofa and become cowboys riding our horses, accompanying the mule train through the Rocky Mountains, where, incidentally, Steve now lives in Denver, Colorado. When I visited him some years ago, we were out in his car, riding through the Rockies and singing this song together. It took us back, I can tell you.

When I was learning the piano in the mid-1950s, my parents insisted I play only classical music. However, I wanted desperately to buy the sheet music to Tommy Steele's '*Butterfingers*', but conservatism ruled at home and my request was turned down. Instead I was allowed to buy '*I Sit in the Sun*' from the musical '*Salad Days*', which was tuneful, but I didn't have my heart in it. I can imagine now those people walking past our house as they came home from work in the evening, hearing me plonking it out on our upright piano. If only it had been *Butterfingers*.

At both primary and secondary schools, there were weekly singing classes which I enjoyed from an early age. Every day began with a school assembly, when the children would sing a hymn accompanied by a piano. Christmas carols were always sung in our house by all four children and our mum. From the age of eleven, I clumsily accompanied these on our piano. Although I was not proficient, I did retain a strong love of carols, my favourite being '*See Amid the Winter's Snow*'.

These are my earliest memories of music – nursery rhymes, my mum's records and classical piano music. There was music on the radio which we listened to every night, as we didn't have a TV. It seems strange now, but families would sit in their living rooms in silence, mothers occupied with knitting or sewing, children painting or colouring and the radio providing an aural focus for their attention with a comedy show or music. I remember listening to '*Family Favourites*', a BBC request programme, which often played one of my favourite pieces – Danny Kaye's '*Tubby the Tuba*'. This wonderful 8-minute story about a tuba trying to play a melody in an orchestra, helped children recognize the instruments and told a sweet story which was brilliantly narrated in five different voices by Danny Kaye. However, most of the music played on the radio was ordinary and strongly vetted by conservative forces at the BBC. This was before rock 'n' roll came along.

The first real 'hook' I remember is the 1958 Kalin Twins hit '*When*', which my childhood friend Diane played continually when Steve and I spent a long weekend with her in 1958. But the Kalins were totally eclipsed by a more talented duo, the Everly Brothers. I just could not get enough of the Everly's music and I think '*Let it Be Me*' is my favourite. However, the only way of hearing more of their records was the radio, as I couldn't afford to buy single records.

Steve bought an extended play (EP) record of Buddy Holly and I loved his clever rhythm changes and lyrics. He produced so much good music in such a short career, before he died in that fateful plane crash. If I have to choose, I would say '*Words of Love*' and '*Listen to Me*' are his best.

It was Steve who bought our first 45 rpm rock records and played them on a little portable record player in our bedroom. His first record was a 78 of Elvis Presley's '*Jailhouse Rock*' and it was followed by 45s of Cliff Richard's '*Move It*' and the Big Bopper's '*Chantilly Lace*'. Steve also bought a second-hand EP of early Elvis Presley which is probably worth a lot of money today. The best loved of Steve's records, by me anyway, were Eddie Cochrane's hits

'*Summertime Blues*' and '*Somethin' Else*'. It was a tragedy when he, who had such tremendous talent, was taken so early, when he died in a car crash while touring in England in 1958.

I love music from the late 1950s. It became so popular the BBC just *had* to play Connie Francis, Brenda Lee, Duane Eddy, Ricky Nelson, Jerry Lee Lewis and from the UK, the Shadows. I liked Ricky Nelson's voice a lot, especially '*Travellin' Man*', on which he was backed by Presley's Jordanaires. The arrangements were so clever yet simple and seemed to reflect the lightness and hope which came from North America via the radio airwaves. I think these must have been wonderful times to grow up in, over there in the USA. I have heard it said art is a cultural barometer of the time we live in. It tries to reflect some of the values and trends we find are important. If so, then in the USA they must have been living in a golden age from 1955 -1962.

It was when I became friendly with my class-mate Peter Hancock in 1959 and I heard his collection of Long Play (LP) records that I started to form strong preferences for particular kinds of melodies and harmony. Peter had an LP of the Everly Brothers and I became aware of how close their tenor and baritone harmonies were. They could swop their vocal roles and could both sing in either register. I loved the teenage world expressed in their songs. We played them time and again in Peter's lounge in St. Mary's Road, Watford.

Peter also had several LPs of early Elvis Presley songs. We both loved these records too, the fast rock numbers were so great to dance to, but even more I loved the ballads. Elvis had extraordinary vocal range. I am not sure if he was a baritone or tenor, he seemed to be able to sing effortlessly in both registers. But it was not just his superb range, it was the tenderness he managed to bring to his songs that captured me. His best ballad for me is '*Is it so Strange*', which I can remember playing on my tape recorder while looking out of the lounge window at the lamplight making halos in the mist – still such a beautiful memory even today. It is said Faron Young wrote this song especially for Presley in 1957 and Elvis sang it with immense tenderness and control.

I only discovered black artists from the 1950s when I was older, they weren't played much on the BBC radio. Sam Cooke had such a mellow voice he was thought to be a possible successor to Nat King Cole. I choose '*Wonderful World*' by Sam Cooke from 1960 as my selection from an enormous number of his hits. I think he and Nat King Cole had similar voices and had Sam Cooke not suffered a tragic early death, maybe he would have grown to sound even more like Nat.

I grew to love Nat King Cole's early recordings, not just for his velvet tones, but also for his superb piano style. I have a collection of his early music and it is difficult to select a special one – but his 1956 '*You're Looking at Me*' comes close. Again, he too died early at forty-five years old, in 1965, of lung cancer.

When I was seventeen, I bought an LP of Eartha Kitt, I was fascinated by her sexy charm and her voice. She sings effortlessly and I liked the range of music she sang. She was fun and I think I liked her '*Let's Do It*' best.

In the 1960s black music started to become more popular and one of the songs I loved was the powerful hit

'*New Orleans*', by Gary US Bonds. There is something in the drumming beat of this number and the powerful sax solos that just does not fade with time.

Another song which captured me was Ketty Lester's '*Love Letters*' from 1962. The melody is so pure, the piano so sparse and the imagery of the lyrics is just, well, wonderful. I could listen to it again and again, even now. Another record I could not get enough of was '*Working in the Coalmine*' by Lee Dorsey. Once again, the drumming rhythm hooked me, as well as his mellow voice.

Then in the middle 1960s two soul singers stood out for me. Otis Redding's voice and style moved me a lot, especially '*Try a Little Tenderness*' from 1962. The other artist was Nina Simone, whose '*I Put a Spell on You*' did exactly that for me in 1965.

In 1964 I discovered Bob Dylan, who I think initially wrote poems to music. I was influenced by his early folk period, but was impressed later when he went electronic. His second LP '*The Freewheelin' Bob Dylan*' included the number '*Girl from the North Country*', which remains a firm favourite from an enormous list of his songs that I love.

This brings me to when I was twenty-one years old and I want to stop mentioning music references at this time, as I must have almost come of age musically. I have purposely not included favourite or influential classical, jazz or folk music. I am sure they are a part of my musical education, but they are much harder for me to analyse to find out why I like them. I know people say there is no accounting for taste, but here I am trying to do just that – trying to ascertain why I like certain songs.

I am sure if you listen to the play-list in the annex of this document you could say, "Oh, this is so sloppy, what a preference for ballads, where is the fast song, where is the fun, what about many other singers who made music during the 1950s and 60s who have not been quoted?"

You would be right, but these are just my personal choices. I have not stopped appreciating music and from 1966 I have bought so much that I love and I'm still finding new music today that I enjoy and get hooked on.

But to get back to these references. First, I notice I have only listed three female performers out of twenty-three performers. So, I guess this means I prefer songs in a lower register, considering women sing in contralto, mezzo-contralto, alto or soprano (going up the scale). There must be something here, all three of my preferred female singers sing in low register voices and certainly are not altos or sopranos. This means I prefer female voices in mezzo-contralto (the most common female voice), or contralto. If I listen to the songs which appeal to me from Eartha Kitt, Ketty Lester or Nina Simone, I think they are in these registers.

Male singers mostly sing in bass, baritone and tenor. I am not qualified to state whether Bing Crosby is a baritone or tenor, but as he hits high notes so easily, I suppose he is a tenor, as I am sure are Henry Hall and Danny Kaye as well. The Kalins, Ricky Nelson and Buddy Holly are perhaps tenors also, although maybe Eddie Cochrane was a baritone. Elvis Presley, Sam Cooke, Nat King Cole, Otis Redding and Bob Dylan can all sing in both baritone and tenor registers with ease. I guess Gary US Bonds and Lee Dorsey are more tenor than baritone. This leads me to think, if we use my sample data as a measurement, I actually prefer tenors over bass and baritone.

I am not sure what all of this means, besides the fact I have a preference for slightly high-voiced male (tenors) and lower-voiced female (mezzo-contralto) singers. Interestingly, I have checked out my own voice on the Internet and find I can sing in a tenor register of exactly two octaves. So now my question is: do we have a preference for singers who sing in the same register as ourselves?

But there is so much more to music than just the voice register. Music is complicated if you dig deep into the theory. I mentioned voice range, but it's just one of eight main characteristics of the human voice. I think I'll leave the theory alone and just say I am intrigued by the originality I find in it.

For me music has to have a strong lilt to it and I don't always like songs with a heavy repetitive beat. I prefer to dance to music in the offbeat rhythm style, which is most evident in bluebeat and ska music. But offbeat music would exclude just about all of the early rock songs I like, so this is not entirely true.

One thing I noticed from this exercise is of all the twenty-three musicians listed, seven of them died young – Buddy Holly, Eddie Cochrane, Ricky Nelson, Elvis Presley, Sam Cooke, Nat King Cole and Otis Redding. Perhaps this is just an indication of the high risks some musicians take when they are young, or maybe the difficulties of maintaining psychological stability when they become famous. Whatever, their songs possessed something unique for me.

It's difficult to decide what it is that makes you like certain pieces of music. What is it in a particular song or tune which captures your interest and makes you want to hear it again? For sure, music is appreciated differently by everyone, so what is it that makes us like a particular piece and not another, which someone else loves enormously? I think musical influences begin at an early age, which is why I started this piece with early radio broadcasts that I heard as a child.

If you want to, when it's a rainy day and you haven't much to do, play the song list in the Annex. Perhaps it could be like Steve and me playing our mother's music sixty years ago. You could catch up with my musical influences and this might cause you to reflect on your own.

Annex

These are the songs which helped me form a particular musical preference. I list them as they appear in my text. They are all to be found in their original form on *youtube.com*. If you want a trip down my Memory Lane, go ahead, log on to *youtube.com* and play them. Remember they need to be listened to in the context of their time – although for me they are timeless. On *youtube.com* try to select the original recording – they don't always have a video/film with them – they were not made in those times – just vinyl records.

The Teddy Bear's Picnic	Henry Hall (1932)
Dear Hearts and Gentle People	Bing Crosby (1949)
Mule Train	Bing Crosby (1949)
Tubby the Tuba	Danny Kaye (1945)
Butterfingers	Tommy Steele (1957)
I Sit in the Sun	Salad Days musical (1952)
See Amid the Winter's snow	Traditional carol
When	The Kalin Twins (1958)
Let it Be Me	The Everly Brothers (1960)
Words of Love	Buddy Holly (1957)
Listen to Me	Buddy Holly (1957)

Summertime Blues	Eddie Cochrane (1958)
Somethin' Else	Eddie Cochrane (1959)
Travellin' Man	Ricky Nelson (1961)
Is it So Strange	Elvis Presley (1957)
Wonderful World	Sam Cooke (1960)
You're Looking at Me	Nat King Cole (1956)
Let's Do It	Eartha Kitt (1954)
New Orleans	Gary US Bonds (1960)
Love Letters	Ketty Lester (1962)
Working in the Coalmine	Lee Dorsey (1966)
Try a Little Tenderness	Otis Redding (1962)
I Put a Spell on You	Nina Simone (1965)
The Girl from the North Country	Bob Dylan (1963)

Starting Work in 1961

I started work as a junior draftsman in Paddington, London on October 2nd, 1961 at Constructors John Brown Ltd, a petro-chemical contractor. I used to take the Bakerloo line train from Carpenders Park, out in the north-western London suburbs, to Paddington, fifteen stops in all. I read two library books a week on the train journey, which from door to door took an hour – in those days I was deep into Ernest Hemingway and John Steinbeck.

Initially, while I was still at school, I had the idea of becoming a land surveyor and my Uncle John arranged an interview for me with a chartered surveyors he knew in London, so I could have more of an idea of what the job entailed. When I met the surveyor, who was helpful, he informed me I would need to study full-time for two years and obtain my GCE A levels, and then I would have to attend university for three years. This was not a possibility for me, as my mum needed me to go to work and bring home a wage, like my brother Steve. The surveyor confirmed there was no part-time route, for example by studying at technical college, to gain entrance to the Royal Society of Chartered Surveyors. During the interview, I realised I was not totally enamoured by the surveying work described to me and, after some discussion, I found what I wanted to do was to design and build structures.

It was suggested I could become a civil engineer and here there was a part-time study route through the Higher National Certificate qualification to become a Member of the Institute of Civil Engineers.

I wrote applying for a job to about twenty-five civil engineering contractors who were busy re-building London after the Blitz. Those who replied were not interested in employing a sixteen-year-old. They preferred to accept graduates. However, through the father of a boy I knew at the Boy Scouts, I got an interview with CJB, who said they would take me on, initially as a draftsman and then, as I progressed through technical college, as a junior engineer. At the interview I learnt that many of their engineers believed if you could draw and make design calculations, this greatly improved your ability to conceptualise engineering structures. Later this proved to be oh, so true. CJB indentured me to the Institution of Civil Engineers with one of their senior engineers, Mr. J.C.W. Barnett, so I would be on the right path to become a Graduate Member when my academic training was complete. And I was paid £5.75 a week, too.

Complete in my new sports jacket and grey flannels, recently purchased from John Collier, and a thin leather document case, which was actually used to carry my lunchtime sandwiches, I started work at CJB on a glorious, golden morning in autumn. I was greeted by Mr. Mooney from personnel, who offered me the limpest handshake in the world – his hand was like a dead trout. He immediately took me up three floors to meet Howard Edwards, a Welsh senior engineer, who showed me to my drawing board and explained, before actually drawing anything, I would have to learn to print. He showed me how to fix what was called an 'elephant' size tracing sheet to the board with pieces of sticky drafting tape. He then instructed me to draw two parallel lines exactly 6 mm apart which I had to fill in with the alphabet A, B, C … in capital letters, followed by numbers up to 10 which I did, using an HB pencil. He then looked over my efforts and pronounced it was not good enough, but was OK for a beginner. He asked me to fill the entire sheet with lines and complete it with letters and numbers, trying as hard as possible to improve the printing. He showed me many examples of other draftsmen's work, which of course, were much better than mine. I was introduced to the men in my section and one engineer, John, was to be my contact and mentor. John was thirty-two years old and I learnt a lot from him in my first days at work.

CJB was housed in a brand-new building in Eastbourne Terrace, which ran next to Paddington Main Line Station, so you could walk through the station from the Tube, up some stairs and then nip over the busy Eastbourne Terrace road and into CJB House. This was a twenty-storey tower block plus an adjacent three-floor building, which contained my drawing office. This was a long room extending for almost the complete width of the building, with windows down one side to let in light and the other side lined with offices for the bosses. The drawing office desks were specially constructed to support a parallel motion drawing board on their rear, so you could sit at your board and then swivel around on your chair and work on a desk with a full width drawer in it to store drawings. This arrangement was repeated for the length of the office, about twenty boards and desks, in three rows across.

So from my board you could look up the office and see heads bent over boards, men chatting to one another and engineers in groups discussing work problems. When it became darker in the afternoon electric angle-poise lamps attached to the boards were switched on, giving a cosy, but industrial feeling to the offices which I liked. I felt at home immediately.

John took me to the stores and I was issued with a selection of Castell pencils and an eraser, or 'rubber' as they were called then, coloured blue and reddish brown. The brown was for soft pencil erasure, 2B and HB, and the blue for hard pencils like 2H and 3H. I was told to bring a yellow duster from home and to buy a jacket overall to wear, as days spent leaning on drawings made with pencil-lead quickly got your nice clean shirt dirty. I was given blocks of notepaper, a scale rule and a long-handled brush to clean off drawings.

Then back to the board to fill in the gigantic sheet with letters and numbers. John paid a lot of attention to my efforts and explained I needed to develop my own style of printing. He showed me lots of examples, those of the architectural team were the most stylistic. By the end of the day I had filled in half the sheet and could see what I thought was an improvement. I had done technical drawing at school, so I already knew you shouldn't write in longhand on drawings, you had to use thin guide lines made in light pencil and print in between them.

The hours at CJB in 1961 were 9 – 12.30am and 1.30 – 5.30pm, a seven-and-a-half-hour day, thirty-seven and a half hours a week with two weeks paid holiday a year. There were no unions at CJB, as the company was involved in the new industry of petro-chemical plant design and construction which had started to take off after the Second World War. This involved projects like gas plants, oil terminals and fertilizer factories which were designed at Eastbourne Terrace then constructed with staff on sites around the UK.

On my first morning in the office I was pleased to find at 10.30am a tea trolley was pushed round by a nice-looking lady, serving tea and biscuits – heaven. I noticed no-one else was my age. The nearest was Stan Palmer, a thin strip of a guy aged about nineteen, who, I found out, was the office joker. I felt young amongst all these men. I had just finished 5th year in secondary modern school where I was among the oldest boys in the school, and now before the actual year was finished, here I was at work, the youngest. It was a little unnerving. There was one architect, Old Harry, who looked like someone's grandad. I ate my sandwiches at lunch and afterwards met a few young guys who were all about twenty-two and were in the final stages of part-time HNC courses, but no-one came from my part of London. They went to Westminster Technical College, or, like Stan, to Acton Technical College. They were friendly and invited me out for lunch the next day, as I discovered to my delight that CJB issued you with a two shillings and sixpence luncheon voucher every day.

I enrolled at Willesden Technical College on Thursday and here they informed me as I had six O Level GCE subjects I needn't do the first year of the course, but could jump into the second year which had already started a few weeks before.

The National Certificate Civil Engineering course was made in two separate three-year blocks – Ordinary National Certificate (ONC) for three years (of which I only had to do two years) and Higher National Certificate (HNC) for a further three years. I was also required to study four separate endorsement subjects to complete the HNC course. The endorsement subjects were scheduled on separate evenings at night school. So as the ONC or HNC classes comprised a full day and also a night school class, with the extra endorsement subject I would be studying for one day and two nights every week.

My company paid me for five days a week even when I was at technical college as their investment in the scheme, so that I could progress to do more difficult work in the office. This sort of education was the backbone of British industry in the 1950s and 60s, as there were so few universities for aspiring young men and women to attend. It worked well, I received practical experience at work and coupled it with technical knowledge gained at part-time school. After gaining my HNC, I would be accepted by the prestigious Institute of Civil Engineers as a Graduate Member. Then, after working under a chartered engineer for a minimum of three years, I would write a paper and have a technical interview on it. If I passed, and as long as I was twenty-five years old, I would be elected a chartered civil engineer with the letters CEng MICE after my name.

The downside of an HNC Civil Engineering course was that it took at least six years to complete, and in my experience, my lecturers were sometimes sub-standard. They were often absent from the classes and when they were present, there was little time for questions. It was a rote-method of learning which I did not appreciate. However, I quickly made a close friend in Ian Mackay, who lived not too far away from me in Belmont, near Harrow. He'd started on the chartered surveyor's route but didn't like it and had swopped to civil engineering and was also allowed to miss the first year of ONC. Mac and I studied together for the next six years, often cooperating with one another on homework by working out problems between us. In this way we managed to get over the chronic lack of real teaching which we experienced.

At work, after three days of print practice I was given my first CJB tracing sheet and asked to make a drawing of plans, sections and details of a circular, precast concrete manhole as practice. During the second week John started showing me prints of piping layout drawings and explaining the components. His team was designing steel staircases, walkways and platforms which were needed to access the valves and instruments attached to the pipes. The pipes served the offsite facilities of a large refinery in Wales and were of varying diameters, some as big as 600 mm. It was a puzzle to add and subtract sizes to make sure a 100 mm steel angle leg could be inserted between the pipes.

It seemed I did a good job. I was good at mathematics, so I rarely made a mistake. John explained we would make the drawing part in pencil and the printing would be in ink. I needed more practice at this. I chose to use what most of the architects selected, which was the mapping pen. CJB issued you with mapping nibs, and I bought a box of matches and used the box to keep all my nibs in and curiously, I still have it today, fifty-eight years later.

One morning, after about a month, I took my cup of tea and chatted to Stan and Seamus, an Irish architect. I did not take sugar, which was served in lumps, but when Seamus dutifully stirred his four lumps into his tea, it turned black. Stan had taken a Pelican ink bottle plunger and carefully soaked black ink into a sugar lump and then passed it off on Seamus. Lots of men laughed and Stan obediently got a new tea for Seamus – I was finding out men mucked about at work, just like boys at school. I would have to be careful here.

Behind Eastbourne Terrace is Westbourne Terrace, a once graceful, tree-lined road. Now, seventeen years after the war it was full of bomb-sites and many of the elegant white stucco-fronted houses were derelict. In 1962 the whole road had become a construction site with only the facades of the houses left standing. Outside my window, on the other side of the road, a construction company was building Telstar House, named after the recently launched Russian sputnik. They were busy constructing the foundations and it was quite fascinating to watch it for a bit, as long as Howard Edwards didn't catch you and make one of his sarcastic comments.

There were two phones on the window-sill, a grey one for internal calls, and a black one for external. There were few external calls but lots of internal ones and I soon realised everyone nearby expected me to answer the phone and then call them over. I didn't mind, we had a phone at home which rarely rung for me, so a few times a day it was, "252, OK, John, phone call please!" or "252, Colin, Pete for you!" I guess someone must have noticed my alacrity in answering, for one day when I picked it up and said:

"252?"

Nothing, no response, so I repeated, "Hello, 252?"

Still nothing and then the response came, "Arseholes!" and then he rang off.

I couldn't believe it, I turned around and looked up the office but no-one was watching me. I mentioned it jokingly to Stan, as I was sure it was not his voice. He roared with laughter and of course, told everyone else. It seemed to be the joke of the day. Now, every time I answered the phone, a few eyes watched me waiting for it to happen again, and I hesitatingly expected it to be repeated – but it wasn't, until I had settled down again. Then about ten days later he got me:

"252?" and then, "Arseholes!"

I never discovered who was doing this and anyway, John moved my position away from the window, so someone else had to answer the phone.

Winter came on and I was glad to be on the train out of the cold weather, in the warm fug of the railway carriage. I was now reading the First World War poets, like Robert Graves's *Goodbye to All That*, having finished all the Steinbeck and Hemingway novels. If I didn't have a book, my train journey to work was rather boring. When I went to my day-release course at Willesden I would get off the train at Stonebridge Park station, catch the bus around the North Circular road and then walk to Willesden Technical College. This journey became a drag. The buses hardly ever ran to schedule and were often late. When it rained, the North Circular was a depressing ride. Sometimes a guy from my night school class gave me a lift to Stonebridge Park station in his car, which helped a lot. I decided to bicycle from home on Thursdays, a distance of twenty kilometres. It took about fifty minutes, but I had to stop doing it if the weather was bad, like snow or ice.

One day in early 1962 there was a train strike so I cycled from home to CJB in Paddington, thirty kilometres. It took me an hour and a quarter.

On Christmas Eve no-one seemed to be doing anything in the morning and there was a relaxed atmosphere. Christmas decorations had been put up in the office by secretaries and technical clerks. Stan explained we would be going to a pub called the 'Load of Hay' for lunch, in Praed Street, Paddington's main thoroughfare. Dutifully at 12.20pm we all left the office early and trouped up Praed Street with its little shops and scruffy pavements. The Load of Hay was already heaving with people and even outside there was a strong smell of beer. The floor was wet with spilt beer and there was almost nowhere to stand. So, we squeezed in and found enough space near the toilet at the back. I'd never been in a pub before, was under age (you needed to be eighteen years old) and was not overly impressed. The Load of Hay was a big place, but not nice and I did not like the taste of my first beer, but in my attempts to appear older I consumed it little by little, trying to refuse offers of refills.

The pub got louder as even more people came in. A young girl squeezed through and when she passed Stan, he said to her, "Hey darlin', how about a kiss for Christmas?"

To my amazement she dutifully obliged, giving Stan a long snog, and then grinning her head off, ducked back into the crowd. Stan turned to us all to reveal a peppermint Polo between his teeth, which she had passed on to him.

"Talk about mouth to mouth resuscitation," someone said.

No food was served, so after two hours and two pints of draught beer, I decided to leave and get a sandwich from the station, on the way back to work. As I squeezed my way out, I passed the cash register on the end of the bar where, just after the barmaid had rung up a sale and the drawer had opened, a drunk leaned forward and was sick directly into the till. Sort that out and Happy Christmas, I thought.

CJB held its Christmas party at the 100 Club in Oxford Street. Ken Collier's Band played traditional jazz at a very loud volume. I loved it, but had to leave at eleven, in order to catch the last train back to Carpenders Park. My ears were still ringing when I walked up the road to my home. The weekend before Christmas, I invited my school friend Peter Hancock up to Paddington to have a Christmas roast lunch with me, in a rather nicer pub, using the ten spare luncheon vouchers I had saved up.

Normally, I went for lunch a couple of times a week with colleagues to nearby Queensway, which was a cosmopolitan area between Paddington and Hyde Park. Many Polish, Italian and other immigrants lived here and had opened little restaurants. I had never been to an Italian restaurant before and had spaghetti bolognaise for the first time. The only spaghetti I had eaten previously came out of a tin and was coloured orange. I loved Queensway, with its Whiteley's store, which was the first departmental store in London. Then it was a big rambling old place full of Persian carpets, cloth sections selling silks and curtains and all manner of furniture. Much of the produce seemed to have come from England's old empire. It was a long way from the sleek, fashionable, modern shopping centre rebuilt at the end of the twentieth century.

We also went to a Wimpy Bar, a new sort of establishment which sold beef-burgers and chips. It was a dark place, with low Formica topped tables and stools – all very different from a Lyons Corner House, which was the traditional restaurant throughout England at this time. Wimpy had plastic tomatoes full of tomato sauce on the tables, which I thought rather fun until I picked one up and squeezed it, to find it squirted tomato sauce into my hands, as the sides had been punctured with a fork by someone. I never had tomato sauce again in a Wimpy.

We went swimming at Queensway swimming baths, which must have been constructed in the year dot – they were at the least Victorian. It had a narrow pool which was rather over-chlorinated but was still enjoyed by us young guys. The tile work was cracked and the changing cubicles were ancient, but it must have provided sport and pleasure to many people over its lifetime. Sometimes we went for walks in Hyde Park. The Peter Pan statue was close to our side of the park, as was the Round Pond. During the winter of 1961 – 62 the Round Pond iced over and we walked out to stand on the ice at the middle of the pond.

During my first summer at work I was sent away for six weeks to Swansea to work on a site where CJB were building a plant for British Hydrocarbons, and then later for a month to West Bromwich to work on a Gulf Oil Ocean Terminal project. This proved to be a totally different experience to my days in the drawing office.

Not a lot of women worked at CJB, just some secretaries and technical clerks, as few women qualified as engineers in the early 1960s. I was rather smitten with one technical clerk called Bernadette, a dark-haired Irish girl, who had a stunning figure. Bernadette greatly favoured purple sweaters at this time, which must have been all the rage. She looked wonderful in them. I had no older sisters at home to make a fuss of me or influence me in girl's ideas and opinions and as I had gone to a boy's school, I had little experience of even talking to girls. However, I decided to ask Bernadette out to see a rock and roll show at the Harrow Gaumont, which featured all the black artists of the time, my favourite being Gary US Bonds who had just released his smash hit *New Orleans.*

I bought the tickets but when I asked her out, she informed me, smiling, that she was engaged and therefore couldn't go. So, I learnt what it meant if a girl was wearing a ring on the second finger of her left hand. Never mind, I took my young sister Vanessa and she loved it as much as I did.

A strange thing happened on the Bakerloo line train one day. I was sitting in a line of seats which were separated from one another by armrests. I was deep into *All Quiet on the Western Front*, when this dream of a woman got on. She was the living image of Carole Day, a heroine of the *Daily Mail* comic strip, very slender, with ash blonde hair, beautiful legs and highly pearlized winkle-picker shoes. And she sat next to me, exuding a blissful perfume. It became difficult to concentrate on my book, and after a few stops I looked ahead, but exercised intense peripheral vision to examine her. She was wonderful and deep into her *Daily Mirror.*

After some time I decided I couldn't let this chance of a lifetime go by – I must speak to her. But how to do this without the whole railway carriage listening to my corny chat-up line? Then something incredible happened. I felt a tingling sensation in my right foot, the one next to her foot. My God, she was rubbing, ever so gently, her high-heeled shoe against my foot. She was obviously indicating in a subtle way she fancied me and wanted me to start the conversation. I decided to adopt a small ruse and 'accidently' dropped my book on the carriage floor, on her side. I was going to apologise as I picked it up and start chatting, but before the words came out of my mouth, I realised it was only her umbrella rubbing against my foot, to the gentle rocking of the train. Oh, the dreams of youth!

In the spring of 1962 I was informed one day that a large number of the staff would be leaving at the end of the week. I couldn't believe it, why would they leave? Not enough work, it was explained. They were not permanent staff but contractors – agency staff they were called then. I had no idea they were not employed like me. They signed pink timesheets at the end of the week, not a blue one like mine, which indicated they were agency staff. I asked one of them, a piping engineer named Bert Smith, where they would find new work. He took me up to the corner of the office and pointed across the early evening sky to a lit-up tower block, some two miles away on the Edgware Road.

"That's Foster Wheeler, the American petro-chemical contractors. Most of us start there on Monday," he explained.

Bert told me that, being contractors, they had no employment security like I did, a permanent staff employee, but they were compensated by being paid much more. And so, at the tender age of seventeen, I was introduced to what was known as the Contract Game.

The next week John explained I would be joining a new team, one floor down in the building. In the afternoon, a chunky, smiling individual leaned on my board. He had a thatch of blond hair which refused to stay down and holes in the elbows of his pullover.

"Dave Taylor-Jones?" he enquired with a twinkle of his blue eyes. "I'm John Gavaghan, you're coming to work with my team next week."

He told me CJB had two fertilizer plants in Russia, at Volgodonsk and Shebekino, and his team was responsible for the layout plans of the buildings.

The next Monday I was introduced to Kevin Neary and the rest of John Gavaghan's team and settled in to my new work. The plants were not drawn on tracing sheets but on waxed linen. The drawing was in ink, not pencil. There could be no mistakes, as it was difficult to erase the ink from the wax surface

I noticed John Gavaghan always seemed to be missing in the mornings, but suddenly at about 9.15am he would appear in his grey overall, with a drawing under his arm, so I assumed he must have started earlier, before me. After a few weeks, I realised he was actually late every day, but hung his overall on a coat-hook on the floor below, with a paper print folded in the pocket and then would leave his raincoat there and come upstairs. Very crafty. His friend Kevin Neary was always smartly dressed and was also the son of London Irish like John, with a crop of jet-black curly hair and one of the squarest faces I have ever seen. I noticed they both filled in pink timesheets.

Kevin was always kind to me and had an off-beat sense of humour I loved. John was a real London character, and once he saw I was reading serious novels, he started recommending me other books, like *From Here to Eternity* by James Jones, Brendan Behan's *Borstal Boy* and Saroyan's books too. He was well-read and intelligent, often getting quickly to the heart of a problem. He was interested in the subjects which I was studying at technical college and asked me if they included reinforced concrete design. The curriculum did not include this at ONC level, it came later in HNC, but John told me it was the most interesting part of civil engineering. He advised me if I left CJB, I should try to get a job with a structural engineering consultancy who specialised in reinforced concrete. John explained in rebuilding London and the post war industrial structures, reinforced concrete would become more and more important, and it would be a good idea if I specialised in it. It was good advice which I eventually took to heart.

John passed a lot of time talking to an older man of large proportions. This was John Katchigian, an Eastern European war immigrant who, John Gavaghan told me, had come from a millionaire family who had lost it all in the Second World War. Their conversation always seemed to be about finance and bankruptcy. One of the funniest guys I remember at CJB was a cockney instrument engineer named Bill Bell. His off-hand comments would crack everybody up. He loved catching everyone out, by saying loudly, "Snowing!" then sixty heads would swivel in unison to look out of the windows, where the sun shone on a winter's day.

At Tech I discovered many other guys worked for structural consultants and they were all busy drawing reinforced concrete foundations, columns, beams and slabs. At CJB I only seemed to be drawing standard details of drainage and roads. After one and a half years, I quit and found a position nearer home, at a structural consultancy in Wembley.

Little was I to realise then that meeting John Gavaghan and Kevin Neary would change my life. After a few years and moves to other permanent staff positions at structural consultants, I still remained in touch with John. When I bought a motorbike, he invited me over to his home in Streatham for a Sunday tea, where I met his wife Daphne and their little son. John started me with some private work, drawing plans for an extension to a neighbour's kitchen and getting the planning permission from the local council. When John and Kevin formed their own agency, called Kenway, they opened a drawing office in Buckingham Gate, Victoria, and a new future opened for me.

The San Francisco Bay Blues

On a rainy day in 1964 I was walking back to my car with the LP record I had just collected from the music shop in High Road, Willesden, tucked under my arm, safe in its plastic bag. I didn't want to get it wet. Not after waiting three weeks for it to arrive from the USA.

A few weeks before, my friend Bob Rowbottom had asked me to visit John Rowe, the eighteen-year-old lead guitarist in his band 'The Clique'. Bob had been managing the Clique for about a year and the band normally played cover versions of R & B standards but to help them form their own identity Bob had written them some songs. His original raunchy 'She Ain't No Good' and the haunting 'Time, Time, Time' were the first numbers the Clique recorded.

Bob lived in Kingsbury, a north-western suburb of London, and had gone to Claremont High School with his neighbour Trevor Roberts. They were both very interested in music, particularly jazz. Trevor played the drums and Bob was struggling to play the double bass. I say this because that's what he told me, but actually Bob didn't struggle to do much – he succeeded like nobody I had met before, so, I expect he played the bass well, too.

We met at his day job at a structural engineering consultancy where we worked as junior engineers, located at Wembley Park just opposite the tube station. I had joined the company a few months before Bob and his arrival changed many things in my life. He took me to the 'Craw Daddy Club' in Richmond which was the hottest R & B spot in London.

At the Craw Daddy you had to have your wrist stamped with a mark which showed up in ultra violet light when you were checked coming back in from the break. It was here that Bob introduced me to Peter Moy, his closest friend from Claremont school days, who now lived in East Sheen and worked for an architect.

The Yardbirds had just secured the Sunday night residency at the Craw Daddy where they produced an atmosphere so exciting some of the young men in the audience would go wild. They would jump up to hang by their arms and feet from the steel beams above and gyrate their bodies to the pounding riffs coming from Eric Clapton's guitar. It was a wild scene, believe me.

But back to John Rowe, the lead guitarist of the Clique. John was still living at home and I'd met him after going to see the band play at a pub in Watford. He was very talented and became the group's star turn when he performed his guitar solo which became a prolonged riff that increased in intensity, augmented by all the other musicians building up the sound behind him. He'd bend over his guitar looking down at the stage, strumming so hard and creating such a sound that the crowd would go bananas, a bit like the atmosphere at the Craw Daddy.

The Clique's dates were advertised by posters all over north-west London and they played regularly at the Lakeside Scene on the edge of the Welsh Harp, the

Railway Hotel next to Harrow and Wealdstone station and the Starlite Ballroom at Sudbury Town, Greenford. These places were home to the High Numbers (later The Who), Rod Stewart, Long John Baldry and many other future stars. Sometimes the Clique were the warm-up band for The Who or the Yardbirds.

In 1964 the Clique was composed of Trevor Roberts (drums), Pete Westgarth (vocals), John Rowe (lead guitar), Adrian Stambach (bass) and John Kitchin (rhythm guitar).

I think John Rowe's day job was in the metalwork trade and Bob was concerned that his parents did not approve of the success of the group and that they would try to dissuade him from continuing down this path. Without John in the band the group's sound would have lost its unique identity. Bob was worried that maybe John's parents were not very impressed with their son's long-haired friends he played music with. Bob explained that if John were to become friends with someone like me, who was studying at technical college and trying to write poetry, then maybe his parents would see this as a more sober and conventional influence. Bob brought the Clique over to my parents' bungalow at Carpenders Park when we had a barbecue in the summer of 1964 and then on November 5th, we had our traditional Bonfire Night and the group came again to let off fireworks and eat toffee apples. My young sister Vanessa was very smitten with them. My wife Bonny, who was Vanessa's closest friend, remembers this evening very well.

One evening, John and I got together in his bedroom to hear some of his musical influences. He liked American blues guitarists like B.B. King and Howlin' Wolf, who I knew already but he was particularly impressed at this time by a little-known musician called Jesse Fuller, who was from Oakland, California. John played me Fuller's 'San Francisco Bay Blues', a song from the early fifties. I loved this number right away with its train-like chugging beat and Jesse Fuller's gravelly voice.

Jesse Fuller was an accomplished self-taught musician who played twelve-string guitar and had invented a support piece to hold a microphone, a harmonica and a kazoo in front of his mouth, so he could play and sing at the same time. Not only did Jesse Fuller occupy both his hands and mouth but he played a high-hat cymbal with his left foot and a fotdella bass with his right foot. The fotdella was an instrument of his own invention which had six strings and pedals arranged to play a cut-down double bass.

Now, I'd learnt the piano for five years and this occupies both hands playing notes laterally on the keyboard, so I had some idea of the complexity of what Jesse Fuller was doing by playing with both hands and both feet. Jesse Fuller played guitar, where you slide your left hand up and down the stock away from your body, while your righthand picks notes with an up-and-down movement. At the same time his left foot went up and down keeping the rhythm on the high-hat cymbal, and the right foot could swivel in a specially adapted shoe piece to enable him to select one of six pedals to produce a beautiful bass accompaniment on his fotdella. And at the same time, he either sung in a deep bass voice or played harmonica or kazoo.

John explained to me that he had no intention of copying this one-man band, but that he was greatly impressed by Jesse Fuller's musical abilities. And so was I, and I really liked all the numbers on the LP, which we listened to a couple of times. Jesse Fuller's own songs were great and his rendering of standards, like '*John Henry*', were very special.

Later that week, while I was attending Tech, I slipped up the road at lunch-time to collect my own LP copy of '*The San Francisco Bay Blues*' which I had ordered. I think I paid twenty-five shillings for it. When I got back to my car, an old Renault Dauphine, I put the record on the roof while I unlocked the door, put my brief case in the back and looking at my watch I noticed I was running late. It was only when I arrived home at Carpenders Park that I realised I had driven off with the record still on the roof. The stupid things you do when you're young.

I ordered it again from the same shop and when it arrived this time, I managed to get it safely home. It has remained a firm favourite for me and I still know many of the words by heart today, more than fifty years later.

I managed to see Jesse Fuller live at a concert at the back of Regents Park in Cecil Sharpe House in the spring of 1965. He was probably about sixty-nine years old at this time. I was twenty. I was knocked out by his performance. He sat on a stool and seemed shy and restrained, but he chatted amiably to the small audience between playing his numbers. What a privilege to have been able to see someone that talented. Although he became moderately successful, this unfortunately occurred at such a late stage in his life that he hardly had time to enjoy it all before his life was over. Jesse Fuller tried so hard to be a success and he left a legacy of music that has now been recorded by great bluesmen like Eric Clapton and Janis Joplin to name only two of the many.

I wondered what Jesse Fuller would have thought about the Clique? What would a black bluesman who was born in 1896 make of five eighteen-year-old Londoners singing '*Smokestack Lightnin*'' in 1964? What might they have had in common? Well, love of music and playing it, that's for sure. Jesse's roots were a lot humbler than those of the Clique, who were born into a welfare state and although they were from working class families, they never experienced the poverty of the southern United States that Jesse Fuller had been born into and which he only managed to lift himself out of by the 1960s. Nevertheless, the Clique definitely felt and expressed the depths of the blues music that was now being played all over the UK. I like to think that they could have had this point in common with Jesse Fuller.

And what happened to the Clique? Well they were successful up to a point. They were signed up by Larry Page and had two releases on PYE records, both written by Bob Rowbottom. Bob explained that for the group to really make it they had to get onto the TV, and that was Larry Page's job. Bob started to miss night school classes as the group's management took more and more of his time. He finally stopped studying and even took a week off from work when the band went on a tour of Britain when he occasionally played harmonica with them. It was Bob who introduced me to that fantastic early British R & B harmonica star Cyril Davies, whose wonderful record '*Country Line Special*' was such an inspiration to British blues singers of the early sixties.

Eventually Bob decided to leave the group to Larry Page – I guess his own role was diminishing. Trevor Roberts left the group and was replaced. Time was moving on and I think Bob felt other strong currents of the swinging sixties that started to pull him in new directions. He'd met Trisha his wife-to-be and became deeply interested in modern art, especially pop art and the history of design from Art Nouveau to Art Deco.

The Clique finally joined the ranks of lost talent like many other bands and now only reside on *youtube. com*. The band was rated well by critics but what was the reason they didn't make it? With groups of individuals it's not always easy to get along. You can't say it was not for want of trying, but they needed more than Larry Page to hold them together and without Bob's encouragement and charisma they probably finally stopped playing. I am so pleased to have known the Clique and enjoyed their music.

At one point during my engineering studies I felt at a crossroads and wasn't sure whether to give it up and spend all my time trying to write poetry and stories. However, I erred on the safe side and kept my day job and finished my studies. I moved away from home and into a flat in East Sheen with Bob and Pete Moy. We held a lot of parties and it was after one that I discovered that my '*San Francisco Bay Blues*' LP had been stolen. I had bought my Jesse Fuller LP for £1.25 but if you want to buy one today it will cost you £250 on Amazon.

I do hope John Rowe still has his copy.

Jesse Fuller was a brilliant musician who took almost a lifetime to become known and finally revered, yet he could so easily have become a lost talent like the Clique or my LP for that matter, broken on the tarmac by a car parking on it. He could have become ill or ultimately discouraged and his music would have stayed unknown. This never happened, but it did for the Clique. What I will never forget is that I was there with Bob and the Clique, experiencing their moments of brilliance when they played their sets in those smoke-filled London pub rooms. For a while I belonged to their time and no one can take that away. It could be the source of a good blues song.

My daughter now lives in San Francisco and she can see the waters of San Francisco Bay from her window. Next year when I visit her, I will cross this inland bay and visit Jesse Fuller's grave in Oakland Cemetery to say hello again.

My Dad's Old Boots

I don't have a lot of my father's possessions, just those maps he left at home and his old boots. I am not sure how these old boots ended up being with me. Maybe my mum threatened to throw them out and I took them forty years ago. Anyway, I am pleased now to have something he wore. But I nearly forgot all about them, hence this poem to finish this book.

My Dad's Old Boots

Down in the garage, with spanners and wrenches,
Lost at the back under boxes and benches,
I found the pair of them hidden away,
They hadn't seen the light of day,
Covered in dust, their heels in rust,
I lifted them out in dismay.

Dad's old boots were lost for how long?
When pulling them out I knew I'd been wrong
To leave them both forgotten there
No polish, brush, or proper care,
I wiped them clean, they must've been
Badly in need of an 'air'.

They cleaned up well and looked so good,
Despite their age I knew I should
Just sit on a chair and pull on that pair,
Seventy years since Dad was there.
They fitted a treat, on both of my feet,
Snug, with a little to spare.

Dad and I had the same sized feet! I felt a little torn,
I never knew him, Dad had died, before this lad was born.
He died in the war, that's sad to be sure,
When you're killed on a foreign shore,
But after a while, I started to smile,
He'd feet in his boots once more.

My brother Steve came and he tried them on too.
They fitted him well – being size forty-two.
His 'new metric' size, now fitted the prize,
He walked up and down with a smile in his eyes.
With the boots on his feet, he looked really neat,
And could barely contain his surprise.

Steve's eldest son visited, gave 'em a try
They fitted him too, in a flash he let fly:
This was his chance for a quick 'River Dance'
To show the old soldier retreat and advance,
Steely heels clacking, the kitchen tiles crackin'
Dad's grandson showed how he could dance.

In town at the cobbler's his eyebrows were raised
When I gave him the boots he was clearly amazed.
"It's not every day," he started to say,
"Such needy old boots come over my way,
I'll soften them up, like the skin of a pup,
Just give me a couple of days."

Now they're renewed, the boot leather shines,
Like a sculpture for all to admire and I find
Their beauty shines through in a sober, brown hue,
Convincing me daily, if only he knew,
Dad would be pleased, with what I achieved
And I feel rather proud – wouldn't you?

Now they're kept in the house, but when I'm in bed,
On nights when I'm sleeping the sleep of the dead,
If the moon's bright and everything's right,
When the roofs and lawns are flooded with light,
The boots can be heard, to dance undisturbed,
By tip tapping about in the night.

Also by Dave Taylor-Jones

Another Side of France

ISBN: 978 1788032 773
Available to buy from Troubador
www.troubador.co.uk

Paperback: £9.99
E-book: £4.99